ASSEMBLIES!
ASSEMBLIES!
ASSEMBLIES!

by

KRYSSY HURLEY

Edited by John Nicholas

Assemblies! Assemblies! Assemblies!
text copyright © Kryssy Hurley

Dramatic Lines
PO Box 201
Twickenham
TW2 5RQ
England

A CIP record for this book is
available from the British Library

ISBN 0 9537770 6 5

Assemblies! Assemblies! Assemblies!
first published in 2002
by
Dramatic Lines
Twickenham England

Printed by the Dramatic Lines Press
Twickenham England

INTRODUCTION

Personal, social and health education (PSHE) and citizenship help to give pupils the knowledge, skills and understanding they need to lead confident, healthy, independent lives and to become informed, active, responsible citizens.
' New Curriculum 2000 Government Guidelines for Key Stage 2.'

PSHE, often considered the domain of secondary schools, has always been implicit in Primary Education and regarded as part of the 'hidden curriculum'. However, I think it is very important that it is not just left to 'happen' or hoped that the children will learn by osmosis and a positive school ethos. Since the publication of the New Curriculum 2000, PSHE has been given the recognition it deserves as an explicit subject.

As a practising primary school teacher, I often use school assemblies and collective worship as a vehicle for exploring PSHE and Citizenship issues. When I first started teaching, staff in my school would spend days preparing class assemblies, which became elaborate productions. These days, as all busy teachers know, there is neither the preparation time on the part of the teacher, or the space in the curriculum, for such a luxury.

During the past few years my teacher's tool kit of books, which provide good ideas and teaching strategies, has become ever more important to me. What I found I really needed was a book of assembly ideas which were relevant to today's curriculum and which I could adapt to suit my own needs. I wanted something which would encourage interaction, role play and exploration of ideas. Failing to find anything exciting, which met my requirements, I set out to create something myself. I hope that this book becomes a valuable part of other teachers' tool kits and gains a place on their book shelf.

Kryssy Hurley

I dedicate this book to my husband
and all my family,
for their enthusiasm and excitement
towards my writing,
and to all the children
who have given me inspiration over the years.

CONTENTS

SUMMER TERM - MY FRIENDS AND NEIGHBOURS

AUTUMN TERM

MY EARTH, MY CHOICE

1. A NEW SCHOOL YEAR

PSHE LINK: TAKING RESPONSIBILITY
FACING NEW CHALLENGES IN A POSITIVE WAY
PREPARING FOR CHANGE

RESOURCES AND ORGANISATION

You will need:-

- A set of 8 -10 Beginnings Cards with beginnings written on them.

SAMPLE BEGINNINGS CARDS

BEGINNINGS CARDS

the beginning of the alphabet

BEGINNINGS CARDS

the beginning of a letter to someone

BEGINNINGS CARDS

the beginning of a race

BEGINNINGS CARDS

the beginning of a book

```
┌──────────────────────────────────────────────┐
│  BEGINNINGS CARDS                              │
│                                                │
│        the beginning of a meal                 │
│                                                │
│                                                │
└──────────────────────────────────────────────┘
```

```
┌──────────────────────────────────────────────┐
│  BEGINNINGS CARDS                              │
│                                                │
│           the number 1                         │
│                                                │
│                                                │
└──────────────────────────────────────────────┘
```

```
┌──────────────────────────────────────────────┐
│  BEGINNINGS CARDS                              │
│                                                │
│      the beginning of a painting               │
│                                                │
│                                                │
└──────────────────────────────────────────────┘
```

```
┌──────────────────────────────────────────────┐
│  BEGINNINGS CARDS                              │
│                                                │
│   the date of the first day of the school year │
│                                                │
│                                                │
└──────────────────────────────────────────────┘
```

- 1 Blank overhead transparency sheet and pen.*

  *This is optional.

- A cardboard box containing the following items:
  a new school bag, a new pencil case, a sharpened pencil, a ruler, a rubber, a lunch box, a paint set, a bag of sweets, a comic, a cuddly toy, a hot water bottle, a cup, a spoon, a toy, a hair brush, a skipping rope, a road map, a tin of food, money, a dustpan and brush.

- Coloured Cards with qualities written on.

```
┌──────────────────────────────────────┐
│                                        │
│            enthusiasm                  │
│                                        │
└──────────────────────────────────────┘
```

2

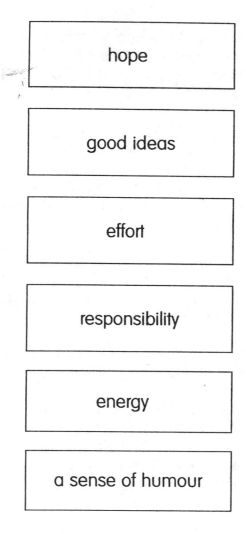

- A set of empty exercise books.

- 10 Children chosen on the day to hold up Beginnings Cards, Coloured Cards and select items from the box.

WHAT TO DO

Start the assembly by choosing ten children and inviting them up. Ask them to hold the **Beginnings Cards** up for everyone to see. Ask the children watching if they can spot a connection between the things which are written on the cards.

Eventually, someone should point out that they are all things which start something or are to do with beginnings. Ask them why they think you have chosen to start the assembly by thinking about beginnings.

Explain that the start of the school year is an appropriate time to think about new beginnings and fresh starts. Reflect upon the fact that the teachers and children have just had a summer break, perhaps some have even been away to another country for a holiday, and now both children and teachers have new classes. There may be some children who are new to the school. Some children will be entering their final year of the juniors, perhaps taking on more responsibilities and challenges, others will be joining the juniors for the first time and experiencing new challenges and different school work.

Explain to the children that they are going to put together a **Back-to-School Kit** in a moment but first you would like them to suggest things which they think are important to bring to school with you on the first day back.

NOTE ☐ You may wish to write these down on a blank overhead transparency sheet as you go along.

After a selection of suggestions explain that you have a big cardboard box which has a selection of objects and qualities inside. With the help of the children, you are going to pick ten things to go in the **Back-to-School Kit**. Explain that there is no **one** correct answer, as different children may have different ideas.

Invite ten children, one at a time, to select an item or quality which they would like in their **Back-to-School Kit** and then to explain why they think it is important. Arrange the chosen items/qualities where everyone can see them.

> When you have your complete kit, ask the children watching to put up their hands if they think it is a useful **Back-to-School Kit.**

Ask if there is anything which they think is missing or which doesn't really need to be in there. Then show the children the things which are left in the box, possibly asking for suggestions as to why they weren't chosen.

Finish by putting a pile of empty exercise books in the kit. Explain that most of the children will be starting new exercise books as they start their new class. Open one of the books and show the blank pages. Explain that, just as it is up to them how carefully and neatly they start their new exercise books, it is up to them how they start their new school year. The new year is like a blank page, waiting to be written on, and it is up to them as to how they want to start that blank page.

Finish the assembly with the following reflection.

REFLECTION

Life is like a blank piece of paper and we are the authors of our story.
Life is like a bubbling river. We cannot see the rapids around the next corner or the beautiful views which await us but we have the power to steer the boat.
Yesterday is already a dream, tomorrow but a vision.
Today is in our hands.
Let us look to today and let us fill it with the glory of action, the bliss of growth and the splendour of beauty.

inspired by a Sanskrit prayer

ADDITIONAL RESOURCES AND ACTIVITIES

> The children could design their own comic strip showing how they spent their summer holiday.

> The children could draw and label their own suggested **Back-to-School Kits**.

> The children could write about what they expect/are looking forward to in this new school year.

NOTE ☐ This could also be linked to their target setting.

> Read or act out New World from Together Now, Original Duologues by Ken Pickering, Dramatic Lines.

> The older children could visit the classes of the new-intake children and talk about their first day. A playground 'buddy' system could be introduced for these children.

> The older children could write letters to the new children describing school routines and codes of practice.

2. GROWTH AND CYCLES

PSHE LINK: PREPARING FOR CHANGE
FEELING POSITIVE ABOUT THEMSELVES

RESOURCES AND ORGANISATION

You will need:-

• A plant bulb.

• 2 Labels which can be hung around a child's neck which say:

PLANT

HUMAN

• A can of drink, a packet of food, a watering can, plant food, a small bag of soil, a plant pot.

• A set of 9 Care Labels which you hold up.*
*or children can hold up.

CARE LABELS

CARE LABEL

care and attention

CARE LABEL

warmth

CARE LABEL

sunlight

CARE LABEL

to be weeded regularly

CARE LABEL

love

CARE LABEL

oxygen

CARE LABEL

to be guided and educated

CARE LABEL

friends

```
┌─────────────────────────────────┐
│ CARE LABEL                        │
│                                   │
│          carbon dioxide           │
│                                   │
│                                   │
└─────────────────────────────────┘
```

- 1 Flip chart.

- Large pictures of an egg, a chick and a hen.

- 2 Volunteers to represent a plant and a human.

- 1 Volunteer to help with the egg, chick, hen cycle.

WHAT TO DO

Start the assembly by showing the children a daffodil bulb. Ask them what it is.

- QUESTION: Can they describe it?

- QUESTION: Do they think it is alive or dead, and what makes them think that?

Explain that although the bulb looks dead and incapable of new growth it will, in the right conditions, come back to life and produce a flower. Explain that just as seeds and bulbs need certain conditions for them to grow into healthy plants, so do children need certain conditions for them to grow into healthy adults.

Ask for two volunteers to come to the front and represent a PLANT and a HUMAN. Put the appropriate labels around their necks.

NOTE ☐ You may wish to give the PLANT additional props like a green jacket or head-dress.

Explain that you are going to hold up examples of things which are important for healthy growth and you would like the children to help you decide whether each thing is important for plant growth, human growth or for both. As you hold up each item/label, the children watching can help you decide whether to give it to the plant, the human or to put it on the flip chart in between the two children, if they feel it is something which both plants and humans need.

When you have finished, reflect on what plants and humans need to grow in a healthy way and consider whether you need to add anything to the lists.

At this point, take the labels off the flip chart and allow the volunteers to sit down. Ask for another volunteer to come to the front. Give this volunteer the pictures of the egg, chick and hen and ask the child to stick them on the flip chart, in the order in which they come. The child is most likely to put the egg first, then the chick, then the hen. Ask where the egg came from . . . . . and, when the child says, 'the hen', suggest that these pictures might be better arranged in a circle as they are part of a cycle. Ask the children if they can think of any other cycles.

EXAMPLE: the seasons, the water cycle, the school year, etc.

Reflect on how cycles form a great part of nature and of our lives in general. In our lives, as we grow, we end one part of our life only to start a new phase, we leave one class to start in another, we leave one school to enrol in another, or perhaps even to start a job.

Life is full of beginnings and endings. Sometimes we tend to dwell on the endings rather than looking forward to the new beginnings. Think about the changes which take place when a small acorn grows into a giant oak tree. Likewise, with the right care and nurturing, we are constantly growing and developing into adults who are capable of making a difference in the world.

Finally, ask the children to close their eyes and reflect on the following passage.

REFLECTION

Everything on earth has its own time and its own season.
There is a time for birth and death, planting and reaping,
For killing and healing, destroying and building,
For crying and laughing, weeping and dancing,
For throwing stones and gathering stones,

Embracing and parting.
There is a time for finding and losing, keeping and giving,
For tearing and sewing, listening and speaking.

Everything that happens has happened before,
And all that will be has already been.

adapted from Ecclesiastes, Chapter 3
the Old Testament, the Holy Bible

ADDITIONAL RESOURCES AND ACTIVITIES

> The children could explore creation stories from different faiths.

> The children could learn about the cycle of the seasons, concentrating on the characteristics of Autumn.

> A link could be made with work on the human life cycle and children can bring in pictures of themselves at different ages.

> The children could look at similarities between harvest festivals in different cultures. This could include baking bread.

> Read the parable of the sower and talk about what it means to Christians. St Luke Chapter 8, verses 5-15, New Testament, the Holy Bible.

> Read the story of the creation, Genesis Chapter 1, Old Testament, the Holy Bible.

> Read *Brave Muskrat* - a story of beginnings for Native Americans and *The Rainbow Bridge* - a story of beginnings for the Norsemen. Both are in *Stories from World Religions*, Wide Range, Oliver and Boyd.

> Appropriate children's fiction with a creation theme: *Once Upon A Time*, W.J.A. Power, Abingdon Press. *Earth, Air, Fire, Water*, J. Heslewood, Brockhampton Press.

3. DECISIONS, DECISIONS!

PSHE LINK: MAKING RESPONSIBLE DECISIONS
          EXPLAINING CHOICES

RESOURCES AND ORGANISATION

You will need:-

- 6 Large sheets of sugar paper or 6 plastic hoops in 3 different colours.

- Bean bags or something else which can be used to represent points.

- Decisions, Decisions multiple choice question Cards.

- 2 Children chosen on the day to play the game *Decisions, Decisions*.

WHAT TO DO

Start the assembly by asking the children if they have ever read a story where one of the characters is allowed to make one or more wishes. Wouldn't it be fun if we could actually make wishes and have them magically granted, like the wishes in those stories.

Ask some children to say what they would wish for, if they were given the chance to wish for anything. Encourage the children to explain and justify their choice of wish.

NOTE ☐ Initially, they will probably suggest material things, especially the younger children, but some children may come up with wishes which have further reaching effects or which benefit others rather than purely themselves.

Continue by reflecting on the number of decisions we have to make in our lives every day, some almost instantly. Ask them to think of one decision they had to make before coming to school and one they have had to make since arriving at school.

EXAMPLE: to decide between toast and cereal for breakfast. to decide which book to read.

- QUESTION: Can they think of a very important decision they have had to make in their lives?

Share some of these.

Explain that you are going to play a game called **Decisions, Decisions.** Two children are going to be asked a series of questions and given a selection of answers to choose from. Although there are no right or wrong answers, they will be given a certain number of points for each answer.

1 POINT • If the children watching think a contestant has made a poor choice or decision the contestant will only get one point.

3 POINTS • If the children watching think a contestant has made a reasonable decision the contestant gets three points.

5 POINTS • If the children watching think the contestant has made a good decision then the contestant gets five points.

There are three levels of questions, represented by the coloured hoops or sugar paper. Each child stands on the colour representing the level they are at and must collect ten points at each level before moving on to the next.

> Select two children to play the game.

DECISIONS, DECISIONS GAME

NOTE ☐ You may wish to add or substitute your own questions.

Level One Questions

These are questions which require little thought and which concern everyday straight forward decisions.

Level One QUESTION 1

If you were buying a new jacket what colour would you choose?

Level One QUESTION 1 - 5 points for all answers

Level One QUESTION 2

If you could choose what you were going to have for your dinner today, what would it be?

Level One QUESTION 2 - 5 points for all answers

Level Two Questions

These require a little more thought.

Level Two QUESTION 1

You see a new girl in class being sent to the wrong room by some other children, as a joke, when they know she will get into trouble. What do you do?

Level Two QUESTION 1 MULTIPLE CHOICE ANSWERS

A Nothing - it's none of your business.
B Think of another trick you can play on her to impress your friends.
C Quietly tell her that she's going to the wrong room.
D Tell the children that they're being unfair on her and that it's not a very nice thing to do.

Level Two QUESTION 2

You see your grumpy next door neighbour drop some money on the ground. You try to tell him but he shouts at you to clear off and leave him in peace. What do you do?

Level Two QUESTION 2 MULTIPLE CHOICE ANSWERS

A Keep the money. He doesn't deserve it.
B Decide that you'll try to get his attention again and if he still tells you to go away you'll keep it.
C Ask your mum or dad to have a word with him.
D Put it through his letter box.

Level Two QUESTION 3

It is Sunday morning and you have an important test at school the next day but you haven't started revising yet. Your friends ask you to go to town with them. What do you do?

Level Two QUESTION 3 MULTIPLE CHOICE ANSWERS

A Forget the test and go with them.
B Say that you've got to do your revision first but that you'll meet them later in the day and decide that in future you'll do your revision at the beginning of the weekend.
C Go with them. You can pretend to be ill on Monday.
D Start doing your revision straight away and when you're happy that you're ready for the test you may go and join them.

> Let the children watching vote on how many points they think each child deserves, depending on the answer given.

Level Three Questions

These questions may be less clear cut, require more thought and provoke more debate.

Level Three QUESTION 1

Your aunt has knitted you a woolly hat for your birthday but you really don't like it. What do you do?

Level Three QUESTION 1 MULTIPLE CHOICE ANSWERS

A Tell her it's horrible and you wish she'd bought you something else.
B Wear it only when you're going to see her.
C Thank her for the present and say it must have taken her ages, but next time you see her wear your favourite baseball cap and hope she notices.
D Thank her nicely and ask your mum if she can drop a few hints about the kind of things you like.

Level Three QUESTION 2

You break your mum's favourite vase but she thinks the cat knocked it over. What do you do?

Level Three QUESTION 2 MULTIPLE CHOICE ANSWERS

A Don't say anything. She'll never find out anyway.
B Buy her a new vase because you feel a bit guilty.
C Own up. After all, it was an accident.

> **Level Three** QUESTION 3
>
> In a maths test you see your best friend cheating.
> What do you do?

> **Level Three** QUESTION 3 MULTIPLE CHOICE ANSWERS
>
> A Pretend you didn't see anything.
> B Call out loudly that he/she's cheating.
> C Tell the teacher after the test.
> D Talk to your friend quietly afterwards and try to find
>   out why he/she feels he/she has to cheat and
>   persuade him/her not to do it again.
> E Tell your friend that you think she ought to tell the
>   teacher she's cheated.

Continue the game until one or both children have gained ten points on the final level.

NOTE ☐ You may find, with some questions, there is some debate as to which is the correct answer.

Encourage the children to see that sometimes in life there is not always a clear cut 'right answer' and that sometimes we have to look at the circumstances and do what we think is best. Not all decisions are easy to make and sometimes we have to consider the alternatives carefully, thinking about the consequences of our actions.

Finish the assembly with the following reflection.

REFLECTION

Let us think about the decisions we have made today, at home and at school. Help us to think carefully before making important decisions and to consider the effects our decisions will have on ourselves and on others. In our lives we shall have to make a series of choices and important decisions and there will not always be clear solutions or a set of multiple choice answers, like in the game we have played today, to show us the way. Help us to look within ourselves to decide what is the best choice and, when we make mistakes, to look at how we can learn from them.

ADDITIONAL RESOURCES AND ACTIVITIES

> Read the story *The Golden Wish* from Golden Myths and Legends of the World by Geraldine McCaughrean, a Dolphin Paperback, Orion Children's Books.

> Read the fable *The Fox and the Billy Goat* * Aesop - The Complete Fables, Penguin.

> > * Moral - think before you act.

> The children could write their own stories involving a wish or wishes being granted.

> The children could role play a number of difficult decisions with a variety of outcomes, in a drama session.

> The children could pick a fairy tale, look at the decisions of the main character and think about what might have happened if a different decision had been made. They could write their own ending with the main character making a different decision. e.g. Supposing Dick Whittington had not turned back and made his way to London . . . . . or if Goldilocks had not managed to escape from the three bears when they returned to discover her in their cottage.

> Discuss how decisions are made that affect our lives and then find out about: Classroom Rules, School Code of Behaviour, School Council, Local Council, Parliament, E.E.C. Legislation.

> Discuss how people can help to make changes in a democratic society by voting at elections, writing letters to our representatives such as Members of Parliament or Local Councillors.

> Discuss other ways in which people can protest in a democratic society. e.g. by taking part in peaceful demonstrations, marches, sit-ins and strikes or by persuading people to adopt a particular point of view.

4. RULES AND LAWS

PSHE LINK: UNDERSTANDING WHY RULES AND LAWS
            ARE MADE
            UNDERSTANDING WHY DIFFERENT RULES
            ARE NEEDED IN DIFFERENT SITUATIONS

RESOURCES AND ORGANISATION

You will need:-

- Bean bags and different coloured hoops, etc. to play the **Team Game**.

- A set of 8 White and 15 Coloured Rule Matching Cards for the **Rule Matching Game**.

  NOTE ☐ You can make up your own rules/situations or use the Sample Rule Matching Cards.

- 2 Flip charts and blank overhead transparency sheets and pens.

- A small number of children preselected or chosen on the day to form two teams and play the **Team Game**.

- 2 Children chosen on the day to play the **Rule Matching Game**.

WHAT TO DO

Start the assembly by inviting the small group of children up to play the **Team Game**.

NOTE ☐ If you wish you can prepare this part of the assembly and play the **Team Game** with preselected children.

Put the children into two teams and tell them that they have to try to score points by getting the bean bags into the hoops. Do not give them any further information or rules. As they play the game keep score, giving or taking away points according to your own set of rules which you have not shared with them. Halfway through the game, start changing some of the rules.

EXAMPLE: Switch from an equal points system to the players suddenly gaining triple points by scoring in blue hoops but losing double points by scoring in red with yellow hoops scoring zero!

Call 'TIME' and give the teams their final scores. Ask the children playing if they thought that the game was a fair one. They will probably tell you that the game was unfair because they weren't told what the rules were at the start and that you kept changing the rules anyway.

Ask the children watching why we need rules in a game of sport.

- QUESTION: Are there any other situations when we need rules to help us?

EXAMPLE: road rules, laws, etc.

NOTE ☐ Make note of these rules on a blank overhead transparency sheet.

Encourage the children to give you examples of rules within their class or school, discuss why we actually need these rules and encourage them to see that we have these rules to help us and keep us safe. Broaden the discussion to include why we have rules outside school and what life might be like without them.

- QUESTION: Who makes up the rules in our country and are they ever changed?

- QUESTION: Can they think of a rule which might need to be changed depending on the situation or circumstances?

RULE MATCHING GAME

Explain to the children that you are going to choose two children to play the **Rule Matching Game**. They will be given four white cards each, with rules written on them and they must look at the rules written on the coloured cards to find a situation or place where they think the rule might apply. When they have matched a rule to a situation they must stick both cards up on their flip chart. The winner is the person to match their four cards first.

NOTE ☐ You may wish to read out what is written on the white cards before handing them out.

SAMPLE RULE MATCHING GAME CARDS

Rule Matching White Cards

Speed limit 30 mph

Speed limit 70 mph

Please walk

Silence please

One way

Do not walk on the grass

Please do not park here

Do not feed the animals

Rule Matching Coloured Cards

on road in a town centre.

at the zoo.

in a shopping mall.

on a motorway.

on a small road running through a village.

on a country lane.

on a race track.

on a playing field.

on a newly sown lawn.

in a library.

> In a school corridor.

> in a shop.

> outside someone's drive.

> in a car park.

> in a park.

> Choose two children to play the game.

When they have finished matching the cards, ask the children watching if they think the two children have chosen the correct situation for the given rules. Point out that certain rules might be suitable for one situation but totally inappropriate for another.

EXAMPLE: A sign which says NO PARKING outside someone's drive and a NO PARKING sign in a car park!

Ask the children watching if they can say why each of the rules were made and who, or what, each one might be helping or protecting.

Sum up by saying that, just as rules in the outside world help us to lead safe lives and ensure that we are treated fairly, our class and school rules are made to help the school run smoothly and to keep us safe.

NOTE ☐ If your school has a policy whereby the children participate in drawing up class/school rules you may wish to mention this and reflect on the fact that school rules are not just there for the sake of it, but have been chosen for a reason by children and adults working within the school community.

Finish the assembly with the following reflection.

REFLECTION

Imagine a football game without rules. Imagine what life would be like if there were no rules and if everyone could do **what** they wanted **when** they wanted, without any thought to others. Most of us have had times in our lives when we wish there weren't rules or when we would like to change the rules to suit ourselves. But let us remember that most rules are there to protect us and to make our lives easier.

ADDITIONAL RESOURCES AND ACTIVITIES

> Children could compare classroom rules, school rules and national rules and think about the reasons they were made. They could also look at rules made in the past, which are no longer appropriate.

> Children could spend time learning new board games.

> Groups could make up their own games for another group to play and evaluate the effectiveness of the rules.

> Read the poem *Chivvy* from You Tell Me, Again by Michael Rosen, Puffin Books and then the children could make up their own Rules and Regulations poems.

> The children could hold 'Mock Elections', devise their own campaign, choose candidates, write speeches, design posters, rosettes and have an 'Election Day'.

> The children could interview an elderly person about changes in their lifetime. e.g. Are changes for better or worse in education, the health service, family life and leisure pursuits?

> The children could research the 'Rules and Laws' of different religions.

5. RIGHTS AND DUTIES

PSHE LINK: UNDERSTANDING THAT THERE ARE DIFFERENT
KINDS OF RESPONSIBILITIES,
RIGHTS AND DUTIES, AT HOME, AT SCHOOL
AND IN THE WIDER WORLD

RESOURCES AND ORGANISATION

You will need:-

- 1 blank overhead transparency sheet and pens.

- A box containing the following objects:
  an apple, a bottle of water, a house key, a book, a first
  aid kit, a light bulb, a toy gun or sword, a skipping rope
  and an envelope.

- A set of 9 Rights of a Child Cards with child's rights written
  on the front and facts written on the back of each one.

- 9 Volunteers each to select an item and find the matching
  Rights of a Child Card.

WHAT TO DO

Start the assembly by asking the children to think about the
most important things in their life. Ask the children to think
about the things they couldn't live without or things which
would make their life very difficult if they had to do without
them.

NOTE ☐ Make a list of most important things on the blank
overhead transparency sheet.

Explain that we are all entitled to certain things in life, even
children, and that these things can be described as our rights.
Our parents, or carers, have a duty to provide us with certain
things to help us lead happy and healthy lives.

Ask if anyone can explain the difference between a right and a duty.

Explain that a duty is something which we ought to do, or something which we have a moral or legal obligation to do. A right is something which we are entitled to.

Explain that most countries' governments agree that there are certain rights to which all people are entitled. The concept of human rights has existed for many centuries, at least since the time of King John, who put together a charter called The Magna Carta, in 1215.

In November, 1989 the United Nations General Assembly adopted the **U.N.** (United Nations) **Convention on the Rights of the Child**. It lays down basic rights for children and helps to protect them against cruelty, neglect and exploitation.

Organisations such as **Oxfam** and **UNICEF** exist to make sure children all over the world are allowed to have these rights, many of which we often take for granted.

UNICEF (United Nations International Children's Emergency Fund) is an organisation which was created in 1946 to care for the health and education of children. Its headquarters are based in New York.

Oxfam (**Ox**ford Committee for **fam**ine relief) is a British charity founded in Oxford in 1942 is dedicated to helping victims of famine and natural disasters as well as raising living standards in developing countries.

Tell the children that you have a set of Rights of a Child Cards with one of the rights of a child written on each, alongside the picture of an object.

Show the children the box of objects and ask for a volunteer to select an item from the box and then find the matching card. Each card also has a fact, or piece of information, written on the back. Help the child to read out the information and then let the child stand at the front, holding the card up for everyone to see the information.

NOTE ☐ It might also be interesting to see if any of the child's rights correspond with the list of most important things written on the overhead transparency sheet.

Continue choosing children to come up and select an item and a matching card until all nine have been used.

RIGHTS OF A CHILD CARDS

RIGHTS OF A CHILD
Card 1

enough to eat

Object 1 APPLE

Back of Card 1

Oxfam helps farmers all over the world
to find ways of producing more food.

RIGHTS OF A CHILD
Card 2

clean water

Object 2 BOTTLE OF MINERAL WATER

Back of Card 2

More than one billion people in the world are still
at risk from dirty water which carries diseases.

RIGHTS OF A CHILD
Card 3

a home

Object 3 HOUSE KEY

Back of Card 3

Some people still have no home, or have to
live in temporary or poor accommodation.

RIGHTS OF A CHILD
Card 4

an education

Object 4 BOOK

Back of Card 4

In India as many as 100 million
children are still not in school.

RIGHTS OF A CHILD
Card 5

health care

Object 5 FIRST AID KIT

Back of Card 5

We take it for granted that we can go to the doctor
if we are ill. Some children aren't so lucky.

RIGHTS OF A CHILD
Card 6

a safe environment

Object LIGHT BULB

Back of Card 6

Organisations such as OXFAM help governments to
provide better services, such as electricity and water.

RIGHTS OF A CHILD
Card 7

protection from violence

Object TOY GUN/SWORD

Back of Card 7

Oxfam have helped teach children in Cambodia how to avoid land mines buried in fields near their homes.

RIGHTS OF A CHILD
Card 8

the right to play

Object 8 SKIPPING ROPE

Back of Card 8

UNICEF helps parents in Mexico learn singing and counting games which they can play with their children.

RIGHTS OF A CHILD
Card 9

the right to be heard

Object 9 ENVELOPE

Back of Card 9

Street children in Brazil have formed a Movement of
Street Children to make their government listen to them.

Once all the facts have been read out turn the cards around
again so that the rights of a child are showing.

Finish with the following reflection.

REFLECTION

Let us think about the duties and responsibilities we have,
both at home and at school, as well as our rights and needs.
Help us to realise how lucky we are compared to many
children in the world. Let us reflect on the following words,
taken from the **U.S. Declaration of Independence**, written in
1776.

> We hold these truths to be self-evident; that all men
> are created equal, that they are endowed by their
> creator with certain unalienable rights, that among
> these are life, liberty and the pursuit of happiness.

Thomas Jefferson

ADDITIONAL RESOURCES AND ACTIVITIES

> The children could find out about the *Magna Carta*.

> The children could look for other information on human rights.

> The children could explore the rights of a child in studies of contrasting countries as part of the geography curriculum.

> The children could research symbolic stories of duty and responsibility. There are many Victorian examples - In the days before steam and modern navigation Grace Darling felt she had a duty to row out to sea and warn ship's crews of the danger from a possible ship wreck on the dangerous coast.

> The children could find out about the many children who worked in the mines in Victorian times until the Government started to pass laws that improved the rights and welfare of children. They could also look at other Victorian child labour issues where children worked as chimney sweeps or in textile mills.

> The children could look up Lord Shaftesbury on the internet.

> The children could find out about the children who took part in the Crusades as many Christian parents from Western Europe felt it was their duty to let their children take part in the Crusades - a series of military expeditions which aimed to win back control of Jerusalem from its Muslin occupiers (11th -13th century).

> The children could compare the difference in children's rights from the Middle Ages to today.

> The *Partners in Rights* pack, produced by Save the Children, is a useful teacher resource and has pictures which could provide useful inspiration in literacy and drama activities.

- Visit the Save the Children website:
  www.savethechildren.org.uk

6. MAKING MISTAKES

> **PSHE LINK:** RECOGNISING THEIR WORTH AS INDIVIDUALS
> SEEING THEIR MISTAKES AND MAKING AMENDS

RESOURCES AND ORGANISATION

You will need:-

- A set of Mistake Cards with examples of mistakes written on them.

- 6 Volunteers to hold up Mistake Cards.

- 1 Child chosen on the day to put the Mistake Cards in order.

- A group of preselected children to act out 2 short scenes, PLAYING BALL and WAITING FOR A BUS.

- Any props you feel the 2 short scenes require.

WHAT TO DO

Start the assembly by asking the children to explain what a mistake is. Listen to several definitions and then read out some of the dictionary definitions.

mistake 1. an incorrect idea or opinion. 2. to misunderstand or perceive wrongly; to interpret or judge incorrectly. 3. to take someone or something to be another; recognise or identify incorrectly. 4. choose wrongly. 5. an idea, answer or act that is wrong. 6. an error of judgement.

EXAMPLE: A mistake is a misunderstanding and also a wrong action or thought.

A mistake can be a misunderstanding - you think you recognise a friend in the street but when the person turns round you realise you were mistaken, or a mistake can be a wrong action or thought - you misread a recipe and use ten times the amount of salt or you are mistaken in thinking that your brother was given a far more expensive Christmas present.

Sometimes we do something wrong deliberately and realise later that we have made a mistake, but mistakes can often be accidental or unintentional. Everybody makes mistakes and it is not possible to go through life without making mistakes.

Ask the children to think of a mistake they have made and to think about what they did about it afterwards. Or perhaps they learnt something useful by making the mistake.

- QUESTION: Was there anything they could do to put it right?

- QUESTION: Did they say sorry to anyone or make amends in some way?

Ask for volunteers to hold up the six Mistake Cards and choose another child to try to put the cards in order of the importance of the mistake.

SUGGESTED MISTAKE CARDS

MISTAKE CARDS

You knock someone over on your bicycle and the person twists their ankle.

MISTAKE CARDS

You get a sum wrong in maths.

MISTAKE CARDS

You accuse a friend of taking your pen, then you find it was in your bag all the time.

PLAYING BALL
Group One/Scene 1

Group One players act out a scene with a number of children playing ball inside one of their houses. One of the children suggests playing outside with the ball but they decide to play indoors, as it is too cold outside. As they are playing ball one of them knocks over the mother's precious vase. . . . . .

- Freeze-frame for a few seconds at this point before continuing.

Group One/Scene 1 Take 1

. . . . . They decide to glue the vase together, put it somewhere where it won't be in full view and hope mum doesn't notice.

Group One act out the scene again but when the vase is knocked over continue with Take 2 instead.

Group One/Scene 1 Take 2

. . . . . They tell the mother what they have done and offer to save up to buy a new vase.

- QUESTION: In which 'take' did they deal with the mistake most sensibly?

- QUESTION: Was there anything they could have done to avoid making the mistake in the first place?

- QUESTION: Do you think they learnt anything from making this mistake?

WAITING FOR A BUS
Group Two/Scene 1

Group Two players act out a scene with a number of children waiting for a bus, when a man walks by and drops a roll of notes. They call after him but he rushes off. After a lot of discussion about what to do they decide to keep the money to buy CDs and magazines. . . . . .

- Freeze-frame for a few seconds at this point before continuing.

Group Two/Scene 1 Take 1

..... One of the children decides that they should at least try to find the man and give him his money back. So they take the roll of notes to the nearest police station and explain what has happened. The man arrives at the police station and is grateful that they have handed in his money. He gives them a reward.

Group Two act out the scene again but after they have decided to keep the money and buy CDs continue with Take 2 instead.

Group Two/Scene 1 Take 2

..... One of them suggests that it would be wrong to keep the money but they decide that they can't be bothered to try to find the man, and in any case he doesn't look as if he'll miss the money much. They set off to buy their CDs and magazines.

- QUESTION: In which 'take' did they do the right thing?

- QUESTION: If he'd only dropped a small amount of money would that have made any difference?

- QUESTION: What would you have done if you were one of the children?

Encourage the children to see that although mistakes were made in both scenes what was important was the way the children involved tried to put the mistakes right afterwards, or to make amends.

Tell the children that you are going to read them a story about a girl called Scarlet. Ask them to listen to the story and think about whether she made any mistakes or just made the wrong decisions sometimes.

SCARLET'S POCKET MONEY

Now that Scarlet was getting a bit older her parents decided to increase her pocket money and let her make her own decisions about what she wanted to buy.   Scarlet was overjoyed and couldn't wait to spend her first week's pocket money. She was especially excited because she was getting twice as much as her friend, Amy, and she couldn't wait to tell her. As her father gave her the money he said, 'Try not to spend it all at once. If I were you I'd put some of it by each week in case you want to save up for some more expensive things.'

She replied, 'Thanks for the advice, Dad, but I'm quite old enough to decide how I want to spend my own money.' And with that, she ran off to find Amy.

'Hey, Amy,' she said when she saw her, 'How about going out for a milkshake and cakes at the café down the road?'
'Sorry, Scarlet, I don't think I can afford it, but you can come to my place for a drink if you want,' she replied.

'Look, I've got plenty of money so I'll treat you. Come on!'

So Scarlet spent some of her money on drinks and cakes with Amy and on her way home she bought a couple of magazines and some chocolate. Before she knew it, she'd spent all her week's money, except a pound.
'Oh well,' she thought, 'I'll get some more money next week so it doesn't really matter.'

That Friday was Amy's birthday and she was having a big disco, to which everyone in Amy's class was invited. Scarlet was really looking forward to it but she had nothing to wear, well, nothing very exciting anyway. So she decided to ask her mum to buy her a new top.

'How about using some of that pocket money of yours? You should have enough to get a top in one of the Spring sales, especially if you use that money Gran gave you last week.' Mum suggested.

She'd forgotten about Gran's money, but it still wasn't enough, put together with the pound she had left from her pocket money. And she still had to buy Amy a birthday present.

'Tell you what,' said Mum, 'If you find a nice present for Amy I'll pay for half. How's that?'

'Fine.' replied Scarlet, who went off to find a present for Amy. If she used all her money and what Mum had promised her she could just about afford to get Amy that CD she wanted. But that would leave her with nothing. Still, she didn't have a lot of choice. She told her Mum that she couldn't afford to buy a top now and hoped that she might feel sorry for her but Mum just said that she shouldn't have spent her pocket money all at once and that perhaps it would teach her to save some of it.

The following week she thought that she might save a few pounds, but when she went into town with her friends there were too many things that she wanted to buy so, again, she spent all her money at once.

The next day one of her friends asked her to go to the cinema with her but she had to say no because she'd spent her money and her dad wouldn't give her an advance on her pocket money. For the next few weeks she enjoyed having extra pocket money but spent it almost as soon as she got it.

At the end of the month a group of her friends decided to go and see their favourite band in a concert. They asked her if she wanted to go too but she only had three pounds left from her allowance. She didn't even try asking Mum or Dad because she knew what they would say but she really wished that she had saved some of her pocket money over the last few weeks. It was then that she made a decision. She was going to open a savings account and put three pounds in every week. That way she could still afford to spend some money but at the same time she would be able to save up for some bigger things.

She decided to forget about the concert. There was nothing she could do about it now. She would just have to look forward to going with her friends next time. She told Mum and Dad what she'd done and went off to open an account before she was tempted to spend her last three pounds. When she got back she was astonished to see an envelope on the table addressed to her. She opened the envelope and inside was a ticket to the concert and a note from Mum and Dad, saying 'Good luck with the savings account!'

Kryssy Hurley

- QUESTION: How do you think Scarlet felt when she saw the ticket her parents had bought for her?

- QUESTION: Why do you think her parents bought the ticket?

REFLECTION

Explain that you are going to read a short poem first.

MISTAKES

We all make mistakes
Big ones and small.
Doing the wrong thing
Sometimes happens to us all.
But if we have regrets
And we care for our friends,
Saying sorry heals mistakes
And helps to make amends.

Kryssy Hurley

We cannot avoid making mistakes sometimes but what is important is how we learn from our mistakes and how we act afterwards.

ADDITIONAL RESOURCES AND ACTIVITIES

> In drama children can be given situations where a mistake has been made. They can role play and experiment with making their own endings up for each scene.

> The children can write stories entitled 'The Big Mistake'.

> Read The Grocer, from Cabbage and Other Scenes by Heather Stephens, Dramatic Lines.

38

7. CARING FOR ANIMALS

PSHE LINK: TAKING RESPONSIBILITY FOR LOOKING AFTER
ANIMALS PROPERLY

RESOURCES AND ORGANISATION

You will need:-

- A large cardboard box containing a selection of objects which have something to do with pets and animals:
  a packet of bird seed, a dog's collar, a cat's toy mouse, a hamster's wheel, etc.

- A selection of appropriate photographs or pictures of animals to stick up on the flip chart to pair up with the Fascinating Facts.

  EXAMPLE: cat, dog, hedgehog, bat, parrot.

  NOTE ☐ All or some of these animals can be cartoon characters like Tom and Jerry, Scooby Doo, etc.

- 1 Flip chart.

- Volunteers to each choose an animal picture to stick on the flip chart.

- Preselected children who have researched and found their own fascinating animal facts.*

  *This is optional.

WHAT TO DO

Start the assembly by explaining to the children that you are going to show them some clues as to what the assembly will be about.

> Say that you would like them to put their hands up when they have some idea of what it might be about.

Begin to hold up objects from the cardboard box. Listen to the children's suggestions. Explain that today we will be thinking about animals, pets in particular.

> Ask the children to put their hands up if they have a pet at home.

Ask the children to suggest certain things which they think are important when looking after pets.

EXAMPLE: clean water to drink, feeding correctly, grooming, being gentle, etc.

Encourage the children to think about both the needs of the pet itself and the responsibility of the owner to keep the pet under control, so that it doesn't harm or frighten other animals or people.

Ask the children if they have heard of organisations such as the RSPCA (Royal Society for the Prevention of Cruelty to Animals) and the PDSA (Peoples Dispensary for Sick Animals) who give advice and help on animal welfare issues.

Ask for a series of volunteers to come up and choose one of the selection of animal pictures to stick on the flip chart. As they do so, read out interesting animal facts about the chosen animals.

NOTE ☐ You may wish preselected children to find their own Fascinating Facts prior to the assembly.

SAMPLE FASCINATING FACTS

- Cats were first kept as pets 4000 years ago by the Egyptians.

- Cats have excellent hearing and are able to turn their ears towards a sound.

- Cats are the most popular pet in Britain.

- Every year, sadly, the RSPCA has to find homes for over 36000 unwanted cats.

- Dogs have been kept as pets for over 10000 years.

- The Chihuahua is the smallest breed of dog in the world.

- Every year about 27000 unwanted dogs are found homes by the RSPCA.

- An adult hedgehog often has about 5000 spines.

- A bat is the only mammal which is able to fly.

- A parrot can live for up to 60 years.

Continue by telling the children that you are going to give them a short quiz about animals. Explain that each question will have three alternative answers, only one of which is correct.

> Say that they must put their hands up to vote for the answer which they think is correct.

NOTE ☐ After the children have voted let them know which answer was correct question by question.

ANIMAL QUIZ QUESTIONS

The correct answers are starred*.

1. A baby hedgehog is called

    a) a hoglet*
    b) a hedgelet
    c) a piglet

2. How many cats are there in Britain?

    a) 500
    b) 7 million*
    c) 20 million

3. A hedgehog is able to

    a) fly
    b) dig tunnels
    c) swim and climb *

4. Bats do one of the following

    a) use echolocation to locate and eat flying insects *
    b) hunt fish
    c) rely on food scraps from humans

5. Which of the following are exotic pets?

    a) a dog
    b) a lizard *
    c) a horse

6. How long can a rock python grow?

    a) 5 metres *
    b) 50 cm
    c) 1 metre

7. Why are exotic pets often abandoned?

    a) they prefer to live in the wild
    b) their owners get bored
    c) they are expensive to feed and to care for when sick
       and they sometimes grow very large *

8. Which of the following should you do on bonfire night?

    a) leave all windows open
    b) keep pets indoors and close curtains *
    c) let your pet watch the fireworks

9. Why is it a good idea to build bonfires as late as possible?

    a) so that there is less chance of an animal hiding in
       the bonfire *
    b) so that it doesn't get wet
    c) so that the branches don't blow away

10. Which of the following are important when caring for your dog?

    a) a brightly coloured lead
    b) lots of treats and snacks
    c) plenty of exercise and a healthy diet *

Continue by reading the children a short story. Explain that you are going to stop at certain points to ask them questions.

ALICE

Alice was a ginger cat and she belonged to Mr and Mrs Jones and their children, Katie and Paul. Alice had been a present to Katie on her sixth birthday and the whole family had agreed that she was the cutest, fluffiest kitten they had ever seen, when they bought her from a local pet shop. Apart from having a pretty face, Alice was playful and entertaining and made the family laugh with her antics. Katie's brother Paul wasn't that interested in pets but for the first years of Alice's life Katie herself took care of her, making sure she had everything she needed.

- QUESTION: Why do you think the Jones family decided to buy Alice?

As time went on, Paul left home and Katie lost interest in Alice and would sometimes even forget to feed her. Katie had a horse now and that was all she ever thought about. Mr and Mrs Jones tried to remember to feed Alice but they were both very busy with work and sometimes forgot to check if Katie was looking after Alice properly.

One day, Katie went to stay with a friend and nobody fed Alice for two days. Alice decided to go in search of food and set off across the street and into town. She wasn't used to all the traffic and a couple of times she narrowly missed being hit by a car. She was tired and hungry, her fur was beginning to look dirty and scruffy and she had cut her paw rummaging through some rubbish.

- QUESTION: Whose fault do you think it was that Alice decided to wander into town?

43

Finally she could go no further. Tired and hungry, she found shelter in an old tool shed, at the bottom of someone's garden. The shed was warmer than outside and there was matting on the floor that she could make a bed with. She fell fast asleep. That night, Mr Perkins, the owner of the shed, found Alice curled up in the corner. He noticed that she looked thin and scruffy and he fetched his wife straight away. Luckily Mrs Perkins loved animals and knew what had to be done. She took Alice to the RSPCA, where they washed and fed her, treated her wound and nursed her until she was in tip top condition again.

- QUESTION: What do you think is going to happen next?

- QUESTION: How do you think Mrs Perkins felt when she saw the cat?

Meanwhile, Mr and Mrs Jones noticed that Alice was missing. They thought that she must have been run over or perhaps she had found another owner. When Katie came back from her friends they told her that Alice had disappeared and that Katie should concentrate on looking after her horse properly now. Katie was a bit sad, and felt a bit guilty for not taking very good care of Alice so she decided to ask her neighbours if they had seen Alice. Nobody had seen or found Alice but she decided that it was probably for the best as she had more than enough work to do just looking after her horse. She hoped that Alice had found a good home and was being looked after by another little girl. Anyway, there was nothing more she could do now.

- QUESTION: What do you think about the way Katie acted when she found out that her cat Alice had gone missing?

After a few weeks, when no one had claimed the lost cat, Mrs Perkins was allowed to keep Alice and take her home to her family. Mrs Perkins' old cat had come from a rescue home and since he'd died the family had missed him, so it seemed like a good idea to adopt Alice, or 'Ginger' as they decided to call her. Sophie, the Perkins' daughter, decided that Ginger must have somehow known she was coming to a good home when she crawled, sleepy and tired, into her father's tool shed. She often wondered where Ginger had come from, and if her old family missed her but decided that, all in all, things had worked out for the best.

Kryssy Hurley

- QUESTION: How do you think the Perkins family are going to look after their new pet?

- QUESTION: Do you think Katie ever thought about Alice?

Finish by concluding how important it is that people realise the responsibility they are taking on when they decide to have a pet.

REFLECTION

Let us think about our own pets and the pleasure they give us. Help us to enjoy them and to take proper care of them. Let us also think of animals in other parts of the world that are being mistreated or endangered species which are being hunted thoughtlessly by people who only care about making money.

ADDITIONAL RESOURCES AND ACTIVITIES

> An animal protection charity representative could talk to classes about pet or animal care or a linked theme.

> The children could give talks about their pet and its needs.

> *William and the Guinea Pig* from the Thinkers Series, TES Direct provides useful inspiration for animal healthcare work.

> Further reading for children: *Trouble With Animals*, J. Strong, Black. *What Shall I Choose?* Church Information Office, Benjamin Books. *Mog The Forgetful Cat*, J. Kerr, Collins. *Some Swell Pup*, M. Margolis, Bodley Head. *Harry's Bee*, P. Campbell, Puffin.

> Information books: *It's Easy To Have A Caterpillar To Stay*, edited by C. O'Hagan, Chatto. Let's Read And Find Out Series, Black. *Animals In Winter*, V. Luff, Black, *Who Wants Pets?* A. Prince, Methuen. *The Young Pet Owners Handbook*, J. Pope, Purnell.

8. HEALTHY CHOICES

PSHE LINK: UNDERSTANDING WHAT MAKES A HEALTHY
LIFESTYLE.

RESOURCES AND ORGANISATION

You will need:-

- 8 Chairs.

- A scoreboard.*
    *or someone to hold up the score for each team.

- 8 Preselected children for the **Healthy Choices** family quiz game.

    NOTE ☐ They need to have rehearsed their answers.

- 2 Shopping baskets and the grocery items necessary for the Supermarket Basket Dash.

- Preselected children who have written and rehearsed their own *Have Fun, Get Fit Rap*.

WHAT TO DO

Start the assembly by telling the children that you are going to introduce them to two families, the Slobrights and the Trimmits. These families are going to play a family quiz game, called **Healthy Choices**.

Explain that the game is all about making choices in our lives, in order to be more healthy. Each team will consist of a mum, dad and two kids. They will be given a series of questions and a selection of answers to choose from. The team with the most points at the end of the final round is the winner.

NOTE ☐ Make sure that the scoreboard is clearly visible.

> Seat the teams on either side of you, facing the 'audience'.

HEALTHY CHOICES FAMILY QUIZ GAME

Introduce yourself as the host of *Healthy Choices*, the family quiz game.

ROUND 1

• QUESTION: Here is a question for the parents only. You are packing a mid-morning snack for your children to eat at school. Which of the following do you choose?

    a) a chocolate bar
    b) a packet of crisps
    c) a packet of dried fruit or unsalted nuts

    Slobrights' answer a).   Trimmits' answer c).

And that's one point to the Trimmits for choosing the altogether healthier snack.

ROUND 2

• QUESTION: Here is a question for the children only. It's Sunday afternoon, the sun is shining and you can't think of anything to do. Which of the following could you do to get a bit of fresh air and exercise?

    a) walk to the corner shop to buy some sweets
    b) play computer games
    c) kick a football around in the back garden

    Slobrights' answer b).   Trimmits' answer c).

And the Trimmits gain yet another point for their healthy option answer.

ROUND 3

• QUESTION: Here is a question for the whole family. Can you name two things which are important in a healthy diet?

47

Slobrights say, after consultation, eating vegetables and a fried breakfast every day.

Trimmits say, after consultation, drinking plenty of water and eating fresh fruit and vegetables.

The Slobrights are certainly on the right track with fresh vegetables so we'll give them a point for that but a fried breakfast every day contains lots of fat and isn't going to do their hearts or their waist lines much good. Sorry Slobrights, I'm only going to give you one point. The Trimmits, on the other hand, gain two points for choosing water, fresh fruit and vegetables.

ROUND 4

• QUESTION: Another question for the whole family. Which of the following do you think are healthy hobbies?

a) playing in a netball or football team
b) swimming
c) going to the cinema

Slobrights' answer c). Trimmits' answer a) or b)

And the Trimmits have chosen the correct answer yet again, gaining them another two points, which makes their score 6. I'm afraid, Slobrights, I can't give you any points for that answer so you're stuck on one point. Perhaps the Slobrights can pick up some points on the last two rounds.

ROUND 5

• QUESTION: This is a question for the children only. Which of the following is necessary for healthy bones and teeth?

a) carbohydrates
b) sugar
c) calcium

Slobrights' answer a).   Trimmits' answer c).

And, of course, calcium is the correct answer, making the score 7 - 1 to the Trimmits at the end of the questions.

And now for Round 6, the final opportunity for the Slobrights to catch up and the Trimmits to gain extra valuable points before the end of the game. The Slobrights could still make up the points gap in our **Supermarket Basket Dash.**

ROUND 6

SUPERMARKET BASKET DASH

And now for the highlight of the quiz and the moment you have been waiting for . . . . . **the Supermarket Basket Dash.** For this, both families are given a shopping basket and asked to choose one member of their team to do the basket dash. Choose your team member now, please!
(Slobright and Trimmit family members consult one another.)

For the Slobrights we have young Jason Slobright and for the Trimmits we have Mrs Trimmit. Now, both teams listen carefully! You will have thirty seconds to put as many items as you can into your shopping basket, but you must remember that you only get points for those items which are part of a healthy diet. You are allowed two items which are not so healthy as treats but if you choose more than two you will have points knocked off. To your starting places, please! (Pause.) On your marks, get set, ... go!

The tension here is incredible! Was that two packets of chocolate biscuits I saw Mrs Trimmit sneak into her basket? And Jason Slobright is heading for a pile of fruit. Is he going to make a healthy choice, I wonder? And, ... (Counting down silently) . . . . . times up folks! Time to empty your baskets!

In the Slobrights' basket we have a packet of crisps and a bar of chocolate, which we will allow as your two treats but gain you no points I'm afraid, and two apples, a banana, a bag of brown rice, a lettuce, a cucumber, a chicken and a bag of carrots, giving you a total of 9 points!

In the Trimmits basket we have four salmon steaks, a packet

of brown pasta, a cream cake, two packets of chocolate biscuits, a bag of pears and some broccoli.

Let's see, that's eleven points minus one point for the extra treat Mrs Trimmit couldn't resist, making a total of ten points. It was a close game at the end, as Jason Slobright made some good food choices and gained some important points for his family, but the final score is 10 - 9 to the Trimmits, who overall made more healthy choices than the Slobrights.

And for our winning team we have colourful **Healthy Choices** pens and **Healthy Lifestyle** vouchers.

The vouchers are for a longer life, fewer illnesses and less disease, strong bones and teeth and the ability to run for that bus without getting out of breath . . . . . but we do think Mrs Trimmit needs to take it easy on the chocolate biscuits.

And our losers don't go away empty handed, for we are sending all four of them away for a week at the **Healthy Choices Health Farm**, where they will be given a bit of help on how to get fit and healthy and have a bit of fun at the same time. And if they let young Jason do the shopping in future we think they won't be making too many wrong food choices. A big round of applause for our two families, the Slobrights and the Trimmits!

> Lead the children in a round of applause.

Finally, invite the group of children to perform their *Have Fun, Get Fit Rap*. They can all do the following chorus together, in rap style. In between each chorus, individual children can recite two lines of their own. These two lines can be about anything to do with keeping fit and healthy.

HAVE FUN, GET FIT RAP

The chorus is as follows:

> Have fun, get fit, it's the right thing to do,
> Treat your body with respect cos its gotta last you,
> Eat the right foods and you'll be looking good,
> Exercise your body, you know that you should!

Children may choose to write a couplet about a food.

EXAMPLE: Mango and apple, I like to eat,
Star fruit and blueb'ries, too, for a treat!

Or children may wish to write a couplet about a sport which they enjoy playing.

EXAMPLE: Tennis is a game, helps keep me fit,
It's fun as well, so I've gotta do it!

NOTE ☐ They may also wish to choose their own props and costumes.

REFLECTION

Help us to look after our bodies and try to make healthy
choices. Think about the things we choose to do in order to
get exercise. Are there any team games which we would like
to play? Are their any sports or activities which are fun to do
that we would like to have a go at in the future?

ADDITIONAL RESOURCES AND ACTIVITIES

> The children could make and evaluate their own healthy
  snack.

> The children could put together a class recipe book.

> The children could look at food labels and packaging in an
  art lesson and use this as inspiration for art work.

  NOTE ☐ See also Andy Warhol's work with labels, *Big Tom
  Campbell's Soup Can* (Pepper Pot) 1962. *Large
  Campbell's Soup Can*, 1964. *Colored Campbell's
  Soup Can*, 1965.

> The children could write scripts and act out their own
  healthy lifestyle television commercials.

> The children could devise their own anti-smoking
  campaign.

> The children could design and evaluate a wrapper or
  packaging for a healthy snack in a Design and Technology
  lesson.

  EXAMPLE: VITBICKS - oat biscuits with added vitamins.
            VITABIX - cereal with added vitamins
            FRUTIBARS - mixed flavour fruit and nut chews.
            RAINBOWPOTS - mixed fruit compote.
            CAROBCANDY - carob confectionery bars.

> Most school nurses will be pleased to visit classes and talk
  about healthy eating and lifestyles. Most area health
  authorities will also have specialist advisers.

9. TAKING RISKS

> **PSHE LINK:** BEING ABLE TO RECOGNISE DIFFERENT RISKS
> AND RESISTING PRESSURE
> TO BEHAVE IN AN UNACCEPTABLE WAY

RESOURCES AND ORGANISATION

You will need :-

- 4-10 Preselected children to perform short scenes that they have put together as a result of role play during a PSHE session.

    NOTE ☐ You can use the suggested ROLE PLAY SCENES or may wish the children to come up with their own situations.

WHAT TO DO

Start the assembly by telling the children that you are going to tell them a story which is based on a real incident, but told by an imaginary character, Jim.

THE RED RAGGERS

My name's Jim. I go to Parkleigh Comprehensive School. My parents moved last summer, because my dad was offered a better job. It all happened pretty quickly really, and having to leave all my friends behind was hard. I'd spent most of the summer with one of my old friends, Joss, while my mum and dad found us a new house and sorted me out with a new school. Parkleigh Comprehensive, it was called and I hated it. It was nothing like my old school and was full of unfamiliar faces. The first day I came back from my new school I told my mum and dad that I wanted to go to another school but they just told me that I should give it a go for a few months.

I'd been there four weeks and things weren't getting much better. The only good thing was Nick, another new boy who joined two weeks into term. Somehow it didn't seem so bad when I wasn't the only new boy. Nick came from London and he'd been to all these really cool places, and he had all the latest computer games. At least I had someone to talk to at lunch-times now. For the first few weeks I'd sat on a table on my own and it had felt like everyone was looking at me. Nick was in most of my classes too, so lesson-time wasn't so bad either.

It was Friday lunch-time and Nick and I had just chosen chips again, for the fourth time that week, and were looking for a table to sit at.

'Let's sit here, Nick, by the door to the playing field,' I suggested. When I think back, I just wish I'd chosen another table that Friday morning. Maybe things would've turned out differently. Before Nick could answer a voice butted in with, 'I wouldn't if I were you!' I turned round to see Adam, from our tutor group, shaking his head at us.

'If you value your life, I would choose another table,' he went on.
'What are you talking about?' I asked.
'The Red raggers. They always sit there. Always have done, everyone knows that.'
'You mean **the** Red raggers!' Nick asked, 'The coolest gang in the school.'
'I don't know about cool,' replied Adam, 'but you certainly don't want to get on the wrong side of them.'

Nick and I moved onto Adam's table just as a group of boys came round the corner and sat themselves down at the table by the door.

'So why are they called Red raggers?' Jim whispered.
'They hang out in the Red Road underpass, just down from Patchley Bridge. No one much uses the underpass, anyway, it's all dark and smelly, and what with the Red raggers always down there, it kind of puts people off a bit,' explained Adam. 'I'm not sure what the rag bit is all about, though. I think it's just their sign or something, I don't know. I don't suppose anyone's ever dared ask them.'

I looked over at the gang of boys. They were laughing and shouting. They didn't seem too frightening to look at, although one or two of them were very well built and looked as if they could put up a bit of a fight. I noticed that they all had a bit of red rag tied to their bags or round a wrist or something. I thought it looked a bit daft really, but they obviously didn't think so.

'Look, I've gotta go, but take my advice and keep out of their way,' Adam said, nodding at the next table. If only we'd taken his advice.

'They don't look so bad. Let's go and join them,' Nick suggested. I looked at him, beginning to have a feeling that we were about to do something that we would regret. 'Didn't you hear what Adam said? They're trouble, Nick.'

'Well, I'm going over to join them. Are you joining me, or what?' I didn't want to be left on my own and definitely didn't want to lose the only friend I'd made since joining Parkleigh. Reluctantly, I got up and followed Nick over to the table.

'Well, what have we here, boys?' said Dan, one of the bigger boys. 'Two curious new boys, I think. You two are new aren't you? Has no one told you about our table?'

'Let them be. I'm sure they don't want trouble. Run along now boys, or you'll be late for you next lesson,' laughed Jon, a small, scruffy lad with ginger hair. I got up and was about to walk away when Nick piped up, 'We want to join the gang, don't we Jim?' I said nothing and the boy called Dan threw his head back and laughed loudly.

'And why do you want to join the Red raggers?' he asked, still laughing.

'A bit of excitement,' Nick went on, 'I come from London and it's really boring up here. There's nothing to do. We just want a bit of a laugh, you know.'

'I see,' said Dan, who'd stopped laughing and was looking at Nick, as if he was considering carefully what he was saying.
'Are you crazy, Dan?' one of the other bigger boys blurted out, 'We don't want them in our gang. We're not looking for new members, anyway.'

'I know, but we could at least give them a chance,' Dan said smiling, 'They probably won't even pass the initiation test.'

The other boy nodded, a large grin beginning to spread over his face. 'Yeah, you're right, why not?'

I began to feel a sick feeling welling up from my stomach. 'Come on, Nick I don't want to do an initiation test. It's a stupid idea.'

'Not so confident now, are we boys,' taunted Jon.
'Yes we are, and we'll do the test, just tell us where and when!' Nick replied fiercely.
'OK. Meet us after school at the Red Road underpass. Just you two, no one else.'

Nick and I hurried off to our first afternoon lesson. Nick seemed really excited but I couldn't concentrate on anything that afternoon. I was worried. I had no idea what the test was going to involve but I didn't like the sound of it. When I tried to persuade Nick to give it a miss he just told me I was boring.

'If you don't want to go, don't go, but I'm not missing the chance to be in the coolest gang in the school. You please yourself!' Nick said, indifferently.
'OK. I'll go, but I must be mad, and I'd better phone mum to let her know I'll be late home.'
'Just relax, Jim, it'll be fine. I was in a gang in my old school and it was really good. And you've gotta do some kind of test otherwise the gang wouldn't be worth being in.'

The afternoon passed slowly. I just wanted to get the silly initiation thing over with. Maybe Nick was right, perhaps I was being silly. The end of school bell sounded and we rushed out and down the street, to the dual carriageway and Red Road underpass. The Red raggers were waiting. How had they got there so quickly? Then I realised they must have skipped the last lesson. I began to get that churning feeling in my stomach again. Nick ran over to them. He couldn't wait to do the test, become one of the infamous Red raggers.

'OK,' said Dan, 'this is what you've gotta do. Take this red rag and tie it to the railing under the road bridge. Pure and simple. You do that, and you're a member of the gang. You first.' he said, looking at Nick.

'But there's no way you can get to those railings without climbing over the edge of the bridge and that's too dangerous!' said Nick, beginning to look just a little worried.

'Well, there's no point in having a test so easy anyone could do it, is there? What did you expect?' replied Dan 'All you have to do is climb over the side, lie down on the ledge and hang over. We've all done it, haven't we, lads?'

Nick said nothing. He just looked at me as if he expected me to say something. I stared back at him.
'You see,' said Jon, 'I told you he was chicken. Come on, lads, let's get out of here.'
'Wait,' said Nick, 'I'll do it.'

The Red raggers looked at each other. They were obviously surprised. I wondered if they'd really all done it. It looked very dangerous.

'No, Nick,' I shouted, 'Don't be stupid. It's too dangerous.'
'Let him go,' Dan said, 'He won't do it. He'll chicken out when he gets up on the bridge, just you watch.'

The next few minutes are still ingrained in my memory. I still wish I could turn back the clock and do something different. But he'd been so determined he probably wouldn't have listened anyway.

I looked up. Nick was already over the bridge safety rail and lying on the ledge. The gang's eyes were fixed on that tiny figure perched on the narrow ledge, red rag in one hand. Nobody spoke. Gradually he eased himself forward, until he could reach the lower rail. He carefully tied the rag to the rail. He'd done it, he'd actually done it!

I'm not sure what happened next. For some reason he turned and looked up. Perhaps something startled him, I don't know. I just remember him slipping forward, arms flailing either side of him and then falling, like a rag doll, on the road below. I looked around me for help, not that there was much anyone could have done, but the Red raggers had all disappeared. I guess they weren't so brave after all.

I'm still at Parkleigh Comprehensive and I've made a few friends now. No one talks much about what happened to Nick now but things were pretty horrible at the time. No one blames me for what happened, but I do feel guilty for not stopping Nick from climbing over the bridge railings. I just keep thinking of all the things I could have done or said differently. But there's nothing I can do now to change things. What's done is done. And as for the Red raggers, they don't exist anymore. Dan and Jon moved to another school and the others are pretty quiet these days. So much for the coolest gang in the school.

Kryssy Hurley

After reading the story ask the children what they think can be learnt from a story like that.

- QUESTION: Do they think there was anything Jim could have done differently?

- QUESTION: Who's fault was it that Nick fell off the bridge?

- QUESTION: What made him do it, when he knew it was a dangerous thing to do?

Explain that sometimes we do things, or take risks, because someone else makes us feel we have to. We sometimes do something just because we find it hard to refuse. Often it Is hard to stand up for yourself and say 'No' to someone, but if we don't feel comfortable doing something, or if we think it is dangerous or risky then it is important that we are assertive and say how we feel. That doesn't mean to say we have to respond in an angry or aggressive manner, just to stand up for ourselves and say what we think.

There are three basic ways in which we can respond when we are put under pressure to do something we don't want to do.

| 1. **passively** | • We can respond passively, which means giving in to the pressure and going along with what the other person wants. |

2. **aggressively** • We can respond aggressively, intimidating the other person.

3. **assertively** • Or we can respond assertively, by just saying what we think, firmly and clearly.

Tell the children that a group of children are going to act out some short scenes. Each scene is in two parts. In the first part of the scene a child is being encouraged to behave in a risky or dangerous way. In the second part of the scene the child makes a response to the peer pressure, either passively, aggressively or assertively. Tell the children that at the end of each scene you would like them to tell you how the child responded and whether they think he or she could have responded differently.

ROLE PLAY SCENES

Scene One

Sarah is being persuaded by her friend to steal some chocolate from a sweet shop.

OUTCOME ☐ She steals the bar because she is persuaded that they won't miss one bar.

Scene Two

Jack is being persuaded to run across a railway track.

OUTCOME ☐ He tells his friend that it is a dangerous and stupid thing to do and walks off to play with someone else.

Scene Three

Mary is being offered a cigarette by Susan.

OUTCOME ☐ She wants the other girls to like her so she says, 'Yes'.

Scene Four

Michael is encouraging John to bully a younger boy.

OUTCOME ☐ He says no and starts to fight with Michael.

Scene Five

Julie is at her friend, Kate's house. Kate offers her some alcohol to drink.

OUTCOME ☐ Julie says, 'No thanks, but I'd love a juice if you've got one.'

Finish the assembly with the following reflection.

REFLECTION

Think about the boys in the story and how they listened to other people, rather than doing what they felt was right. Help us to stand up for ourselves and to resist pressure to do things which we don't want to do, or which we know are wrong.

ADDITIONAL RESOURCES AND ACTIVITIES

> The children could design and draw their own BE ASSERTIVE posters.

BE ASSERTIVE

> The beginning of a story about someone who takes a risk could be presented to the children in storyboard form. The children could then discuss what they think is happening in the pictures and make up their own endings.

> The children could employ ICT skills by taking pictures with a digital camera to tell their own stories. These stories could then be put together in book form.

> Read the short monologue *A Game of Chicken* from The Sieve and Other Scenes by Heather Stephens, Dramatic Lines.

> Read the children Aesop's fable *The Two Frogs*.

THE TWO FROGS

Two frogs lived together in the same pond. The pond dried up under the heat of the summer sun and so they left it and set off together to look for another home. As they hopped along they happened to pass a deep well full of water, on seeing this one of the frogs said to the other, 'Why don't we hop into this well and make it our new home? The other frog replied cautiously, 'But supposing the well dries up like the pond did! How could we get out of the well again if the water level goes down and leaves us stranded at the bottom?

* Moral - Don't do anything without thinking carefully about the consequences.

> Discuss how our planet is at risk through pollution. e.g. human waste, industrial waste, radio-active waste, exhaust fumes, insecticides, ozone layer damage.

> Discuss how we can minimise the risk of pollution. e.g. use lead free petrol, use ozone friendly aerosols, use biodegradable bags.

> The children could find out why the prehistoric animals became extinct.

10. LOOKING AFTER OUR ENVIRONMENT

PSHE LINK: TAKING RESPONSIBILITY FOR THE ENVIRONMENT
AND WORLD RESOURCES
AND MAKING RESPONSIBLE CHOICES

RESOURCES AND ORGANISATION

You will need:-

- A classroom litter bin filled with some typical classroom rubbish.

  NOTE ☐ You may wish to add items of your own to the litter bin to illustrate the point.

- 1 Flip chart with 2 tally charts.*
  * This is optional and is dependent on time and the co-operation of a class of children.

  1. A tally chart of all the litter thrown out by the class at home over a period of one week.

  2. A tally chart showing which pieces of litter were recycled.

- 7 Fact-file Cards with written or printed headings and information on the back.

- 7 Children chosen on the day to each select and hold up a Fact-file Card.

- Threat Cards for the **Tiger Roars Game.**

- Bean bags or ropes for the **Tiger Roars Game.**

- 20 Children preselected or chosen on the day to play the **Tiger Roars Game.**

- Preselected children to read their *'All I want for the world is .... '* poems/prayers written in class.

WHAT TO DO

Start the assembly by asking the children what they understand by the word environment. Listen to their suggestions and ideas, then explain that the word environment basically describes our surroundings.

environment   1. surroundings and conditions affecting people's lives. 2. all the conditions, circumstances, and influences surrounding, and affecting the development of plants and animals.

Explain that we are going to be thinking about how we can improve our own school environment and then consider how mankind affects the environment in general. Ask the children to suggest ways in which we can keep our school environment a safe and attractive place to work and play in.

- QUESTION: Can they suggest any improvements we could make?

Ask them what kind of things spoil the environment. Someone will probably suggest litter as one of the factors affecting the school environment. At this point, tell the children that you are going to empty the contents of a classroom bin, so that they can see what has been thrown away in just one day in a classroom. As you empty the bin ask them to think about which items could be recycled or reused, and if there are any items which they think were thrown away unnecessarily.

EXAMPLE: a piece of paper used on one side only.

When you have emptied the bin, ask the children to comment on the rubbish they have seen.

NOTE □ This activity may fit in with a Science or Environmental study.

At this point you may wish to talk about recycling and stress how precious the world's resources are. You may wish to make a pile of the items which can be recycled or reused.

NOTE ☐ An optional additional activity would be to show the two tally charts demonstrating the amount of rubbish produced and recycled by all the members of a class and their families.

Continue by reflecting on how important it is that we also look after environments found outside our school. Ask the children to suggest ways in which we can care for our planet and conserve its many different habitats.

Explain to them that as many natural habitats are destroyed the animals which live in them are also suffering, becoming endangered or even extinct. A habitat provides an animal with shelter and camouflage, food and water. Explain that you are going to put together a fact-file of an endangered animal.

> Say that you would like the children to put their hands up when they think they have guessed what it is.

Explain that he fact-file headings are written on cards and you will choose one child at a time to select a card at random and hold it up, while you read out some information.

FACT-FILE CARDS

FACT-FILE CARD **1**

size

FACT-FILE CARD **Information**

They can reach up to 3 metres in length.

FACT-FILE CARD **2**

weight

FACT-FILE CARD **Information**

They weigh between 180 and 260 kg.

FACT-FILE CARD **3**

description

FACT-FILE CARD **Information**

They are the largest members of the felid family. There were once eight subspecies but three are already extinct.

FACT-FILE CARD **4**

countries of origin

FACT-FILE CARD **Information**

India, Manchuria, China, Indonesia and Russia.

FACT-FILE CARD **5**

habitat

FACT-FILE CARD **Information**

It varies widely, from tropical rain forests to snow covered coniferous and deciduous forests and from mangrove swamps to drier forests.

FACT-FILE CARD 6

behaviour

FACT-FILE CARD **Information**

They are solitary hunters.

FACT-FILE CARD **7**

offspring

FACT-FILE CARD **Information**

The average litter size is two to three cubs.

> When all the information has been read out, count the number of raised hands. See how many children guessed correctly.

Tell the children that the endangered animal being described is the tiger.

NOTE ☐ You may also wish to give the children an update on the populations of the subspecies which are not yet extinct.

Next explain that you are going to choose twenty children to play the **Tiger Roars Game.**

> Choose the twenty children.

NOTE ☐ Or you may wish to use a group of preselected children who have played the game before.

TIGER ROARS GAME

Mark off two separate areas, using bean bags or ropes, with a space in between. Five of the children can stand in one area. These children are tigers. The other fifteen can stand in the other area and represent the things which the tigers need to survive. i.e. food, water, trees and vegetation for shelter.

When the tigers are looking for food they must put one hand on their stomach, when they are looking for water they must put both hands to their mouth and when they are looking for shelter they must put one hand on top of their head.

HAND SIGNALS

- **food** - put one hand on the stomach
- **water** - put both hands to the mouth
- **shelter** - put one hand on top of the head

The game is played in a series of rounds. At the start of each round the children stand in their allocated areas, facing away from each other. The tigers each decide what they are looking for in that round and make the appropriate hand signal. The children who represent the tigers' needs also decide what they are each going to represent in that round and use the same signals.

On the teacher's signal the children all turn round. The tigers must find a child on the other side who has the same signal and can therefore provide them with what they need. If a tiger succeeds in finding water/shelter/food it can take the child representing that need back to the tigers side to become another tiger. This represents the tiger finding what it needs in the habitat and continuing to reproduce. If the tiger cannot find what it needs in a round it dies and joins the children on the habitat side.

As you play several rounds of this game the children will see that the tiger population naturally rises and falls. At this point you can start to introduce the Threat Cards.

THREAT CARDS

THREAT CARD
drought

THREAT CARD
forest fire

THREAT CARD
hunter

THREAT CARD
logger

THREAT CARD
farmer

If the Drought Card is held up any tiger looking for water dies and any tiger seeking shelter dies when the Forest Fire Card is held up, and so on.

The occasional Forest Fire Card or Drought Card will limit the water and shelter available but this will not have a long lasting effect on the tiger population.

However, regularly introducing a Hunter Card will remove a tiger permanently from the game each time, and a Logger Card or Farmer Card will also permanently remove a tiger seeking shelter. The tiger population will soon start to noticeably decrease. When there is only one tiger left he/she must shout **'Tiger roars'** and the game is over.

This game should show the children that the tiger population can cope with natural fluctuations but the effect humans have on their habitat can be more threatening and have a lasting effect.

REFLECTION

Finish the assembly by asking a small preselected group of children to read out their own prayers/poems about the environment. These can contain the children's thoughts on how mankind can take better care of the environment.

NOTE ☐ If this assembly is taken at the end of the Autumn term the prayers and poems can be entitled, *'All I want for the world at Christmas is . . . . . '*

ADDITIONAL RESOURCES AND ACTIVITIES

> The children could investigate what is thrown away in their classroom in one week. They could sort, bag up and label the litter each day in line with the school Health and Safety policy and produce a cumulative graph on the computer. They could then think about how this amount of litter could be reduced.

> A visit could be made to a waste disposal site.

> The children could design and make a recycling bin.

> A useful teacher resource with a good selection of appropriate classroom activities is *Citizenship For The Future* by David Hicks, produced for the WWF.

> Another useful resource with literacy links is *A Different Story* produced by the Development Education Centre in Birmingham, available through Oxfam.

> The children could discuss the ways in which people pollute the environment: oil spillage at sea, chemical pollution of rivers and the air, noise, smoke and rubbish. They could also talk about ways that pollution can be reduced immediately and in the future: creating less rubbish, recycling, greater care taken with chemical use, smokeless and nuclear free zones and government action.

> The children could design and make a 'rubbish monster' using reclaimed material. The children could collect litter themselves and make models using cardboard tubes, empty boxes, drink cans, ring pulls, etc.

> All religions have creation stories. The children could find out how many religions have stories about how the world was spoilt by humans.

> The children could find out about the world's endangered species - the tiger, giant panda and whale. Greenpeace The WWF (World Wildlife Fund), Friends of the Earth and Christian Aid can supply useful resource material.

> There is a useful website with teacher resources for exploring environmental issues.

> • Visit the website: **www.tidec.org.uk**

> Further reading for children: *Dinosaurs And All That Rubbish*, M. Foreman, Hamish Hamilton. *Where Are You Duck*, Church Information Office, Benjamin Books. *Hunter And His Dog*, B. Wildsmith, Oxford University Press.

> An interesting short monologue is *Turtle Island* from the book Alone In My Room, Ken Pickering, Dramatic Lines.

11. LET'S GET ORGANISED

> PSHE LINK: DEVELOPING CONFIDENCE
> RESPONSIBILITY

RESOURCES AND ORGANISATION

You will need:-

- 1 Large handkerchief with four knots tied in it.

- 1 Table and chair with a pen, paper and sharp scissors neatly arranged on it.

- 1 table and chair with a box containing an assortment of items:
    pens - most of which don't work, pencils without points and various other bits and pieces, scraps of paper in a wide variety of shapes and sizes and a pair of very blunt scissors.

- 1 Flip chart and pens.

- 2 Children chosen on the day to carry out the CUTTING OUT TASK of drawing around a hand and cutting out the shape.

- Preselected children to show the planners, calendars and organisers that they have made in class.

WHAT TO DO

Start the assembly by producing a handkerchief with several knots tied in it. Explain that you have tied the knots in the handkerchief to remind you of the things you wanted to talk about. But the terrible thing is you can't remember what the knots were supposed to remind you of!

Ask the children if they can think of a better system to help you remember.

- QUESTION: How do **they** remember important things?

Listen to their suggestions. These may include making lists, using a diary or organiser, relying on mum or dad to remind them, and so on.

> Next, invite two children up to carry out a simple task.

CUTTING OUT TASK

Seat the children in two separate places, giving one the nicely organised table with all the necessary equipment laid out and presenting the other child with the messy box of mixed up resources. Tell them both you would like each of them to draw around one of their hands and then cut the shape out. The child working at the organised work area will, no doubt, do this quite quickly, whilst the other child will take much longer.

Ask the children watching why one of the children completed the job more quickly. They will probably tell you that the first child had all the equipment tidy and organised.

Explain that today's assembly is all about being organised. Ask the children why they think it helps to be organised. i.e. It saves time and worry and sometimes can even save you money.

- QUESTION: What kind of qualities do they think someone needs if he/she is going to be organised?

NOTE ☐ As they make suggestions write these on the flip chart.

- QUESTION: When do they need to be organised?

- QUESTION: What kind of things do they need to remember?

NOTE ☐ Again, make a note of these on the flip chart.

> Ask the children to put their hands up if they think they could perhaps be more organised sometimes.

- QUESTION: Do they think people can learn to be organised?

• QUESTION: What might help us be organised?

EXAMPLE: make a list, decide what is the most important job and do that first, keep things tidy.

Explain that you are going to tell them a story about a girl who wasn't very well organised.

THE GIRL WHO MUDDLED ALONG

Jade was hopelessly disorganised. She was forever losing things and she often forgot where she was supposed to be. I expect you know someone who is like Jade, most of us do. However, she was a happy girl and it didn't really worry her that she was disorganised. It was just the way she was. She just kind of drifted through life but was quite happy that way.

Sometimes her friends would get a bit annoyed with her, if she forgot to meet them somewhere or borrowed something and then lost it but, by now, they all knew how disorganised she was. And, anyway, if they arranged to meet her they knew very well she would be late so they always told her to meet them at a slightly earlier time. And nobody ever lent her anything really important or very valuable because they knew that she was quite likely to lose it.

However, as Jade got older the fact that she was forgetful and disorganised seemed to get her into more trouble. Her teachers would get cross with her when she forgot her homework or lost her games kit. And nobody ever asked her to be in their group for projects because they knew what she was like. Jade began to think to herself that maybe she really should start to get more organised. But she was so used to letting things muddle along and allowing other people to take responsibility that she wasn't really sure how she should go about it.

One evening she'd arranged to meet her friends at the cinema to see a new film. She was really looking forward to it.

'Yes,' she thought, 'I'm all organised. If I leave the house at seven, I'll be at the cinema in plenty of time for the film at seven thirty. Being organised - easy!'

73

But it didn't quite work out like that. She didn't leave the house at seven because she had promised her mum she'd feed the dog and tidy her room and by the time she'd finished it was quarter past seven. And then halfway down her road she realised she'd forgotten her purse and that she really should take an umbrella because it looked like it was going to rain.

When she got to the cinema her friends were not very happy because the film was just starting and all the best seats were gone. Even though they'd asked her to meet them at seven thirty it was now ten past eight and they were not very pleased with her. But, eventually, they managed to find some reasonable seats and she bought them all popcorn and said she was really very sorry and that she was going to try to be more organised next time.

Well, she tried. But the next day her mum had to give her a lift to school as she'd missed the bus. And then she realised she'd left her maths homework at home and forgotten to bring in the CD that she'd borrowed off her friend, Alison. 'Never mind,' she thought, 'I will get organised. It can't be that difficult.'

That lunch-time the drama teacher was auditioning parts for the school play. The audition for the part she wanted was between twelve thirty and one o'clock. She had her lunch in the school cafeteria at twelve, thinking it would give her plenty of time to get to the audition. She sat at the dining table casually munching her peanut and pickle sandwiches, thinking of how she could be more organised. She decided she would make a list at the beginning of each day and try to allow herself more time for things so that she was never late. At that moment her thoughts were interrupted as the school secretary walked up to her table.

'I've got your maths homework here, Jade. You're very lucky. Your mum has just brought it in for you. Mr Jones is in his room now. I would go and give it to him now while he's still there **and** before you forget.'

'Yes, I will. Thank you, Mrs Lewis.'

Jade looked at her watch. It was half past already. She didn't want to miss the audition. She would just pop along and give Mr Jones the homework and then rush to the audition. So she hurried along to the maths block. Mr Jones was sitting at his desk, looking at the homework. She thought maybe she could just put it on his desk and be off, but he asked her to sit down. He then proceeded to give her an extremely long and 'she'd heard-it-all-before' lecture about taking responsibility and being organised. And she couldn't really think of anything to say because she'd had this discussion so many times before with her other teachers.

Anyway by the time he'd finished talking it was ten minutes to one and by the time she got to the drama studio the auditions were over and the part had been given to someone else. Her drama teacher said it was a pity Jade had missed the audition because she would have been just right for the part. Jade felt like crying. She felt like sobbing pathetically, but she didn't. She knew it was nobody's fault but her own that she'd missed the audition. The awful thing was, she **really** wanted that part. And she knew that she'd have been really good. But it was too late.

When Jade woke up the next morning she still felt miserable and cross with herself for missing the audition. But she also felt a bit different. The night before she'd written herself a list of all the things she had to do before school and she'd set her alarm to go off half an hour earlier. Her mum was very surprised to see her get up so early and even more surprised when she left the house five minutes early. She arrived at school on time **and** with all the books and research she needed for her history project. She was so organised that she was the first one to finish her work that morning. Her friends were beginning to wonder what had happened to her. Mr Cleeve, her history teacher, was pretty surprised too.

Just then, Mrs Lewis, the secretary, knocked at the door, wanting a volunteer to show a visitor around the school. Mr Cleeve said, 'How about you, Jade, seeing as you were first to finish?' Mrs Lewis raised her eyebrows and looked as if she was about to say something but thought better of it.

'Come along then, Jade. We don't want to keep him waiting.'

Well, Jade had never been asked to show anyone around the school before and she was very excited, especially when the

Well, Jade had never been asked to show anyone around the school before and she was very excited, especially when the gentleman explained that he worked in television advertising. Jade showed him around explaining what everything was and where everything was. She liked him and they seemed to get on very well.

At the end of the tour he told her that one of the reasons he'd come to the school was to find a small number of children to take part in a television commercial. After talking to her, he felt that she would probably be suitable for one of the parts. He couldn't promise anything but if she could make an audition at two o'clock that afternoon he thought she stood a good chance.

Jade was overjoyed. She wanted to jump up and down and scream and shout. But she didn't. She was so glad she'd been chosen to show him around the school, and that was all because she'd finished her work early. So being organised had its advantages. She smiled. She was beginning to think she actually liked being organised.

To cut a long story short, Jade went to the audition, and arrived on time. Well! ten minutes early actually, and she got one of the parts. And today she is a successful television actress. Her friends are always impressed at how well organised she is. And old friends who knew her at school say to her, 'You're so organised! You must find it really hard!' And she says, 'Not really. I've found being organised works.'

Kryssy Hurley

Ask the children what they think made Jade change the way she was and become more organised.

Explain that some children have been thinking about being organised and have made their own planners, calendars and organisers. A group of preselected children can come to the front and show samples. The children can explain how their planners work and why they designed them in a certain way.

NOTE ☐ Or the children can hold up their designs whilst you talk about them.

Ask the children watching if any of them have a weekly planner, calendar or organiser which they find useful.

Finish the assembly with the following reflection.

REFLECTION

Let us think about Jade, the girl in the story, and how being organised changed her life. Help us to think for ourselves, be organised and take responsibility for our lives. Try to think of one simple way in which you can be more organised, whether it is tidying up your bedroom at home or getting your homework done on time.

ADDITIONAL RESOURCES AND ACTIVITIES

> The children could read appropriate fables like *The Farmer's Daughter* and *The Miller, his Son and their Donkey* from The Best of Aesop's Fables, Walker Books.

> The children could write their own fables or stories about being well organised.

> The children could design weekly planners which could be used by other children. They could then ask another class or group to use and evaluate the planners, feeding back to them how useful and user-friendly they were.

> The children could choose words which reflect order and chaos and display them.

> The children could look at creation stories from different religions to see how the organised natural world is explained.

12. MY COMMUNITY

PSHE LINK: PARTICIPATING IN SCHOOL AND LOCAL
COMMUNITY LIFE
LEARNING ABOUT JOBS DONE BY PEOPLE
THEY KNOW

RESOURCES AND ORGANISATION

You will need:-

- Preselected children to give short talks about people in the local community that they have interviewed.

- An invited visitor from a local charity.

- 1 Flip chart with the heading MY COMMUNITY and pens.

WHAT TO DO

Start the assembly by explaining to the children that they are going to be thinking about communities. Ask the children if any of them can explain what a community is. After listening to a few suggestions, explain that a community is a group of people who have something in common.

EXAMPLE: we are all part of the school community.

Ask the children if they can think of any other communities.

EXAMPLE: Towns and villages are communities. There are religious communities. You might talk about a business community, and so on.

community   1. a) all the people living in a particular place. e.g. villagers living in a village. b). the locality where the people live. e.g. the village. 2. a) the condition of living with others. b) friendly association. 3. Fellowship - a body of people having a religion or profession in common. e.g. Buddhists, lawyers. 4. a group of people living together as a smaller unit within a larger having interests or work in common e.g. a school community. 5. a monastic or socialist body practising common ownership. e.g. the Poor Clares - an order of Franciscan nuns, Communists, Marxists. 6. society in general, the public. 7. a group of nations held together by common traditions, political or economic interests e.g. the European Union.

NOTE ☐ The definition of ecology.

> **ecology** - a community of animals and plants living together in the same area and having close interactions - especially through food relationships.

Explain that communities are made up of people who work together, live together or perhaps share some common interest or belief. Communities often agree to behave in certain acceptable ways or to believe in the same things.

Today you would like to start by thinking a little about the school community.

> Turn a new page over on the flip chart showing the heading MY COMMUNITY.

Ask the children who they think is important in the school community.

NOTE ☐ As they make suggestions, write these on the flip chart.

Encourage the children to think beyond the teachers and pupils, to all the other people who are part of the school community, and necessary in order for the school to run smoothly.

EXAMPLE: the caretaker, the cooks, the mums and dads who help at the school fête, etc.

Go on to say that you would now like to think not just about the school community, but about a wider local community. Ask if any of the children are involved in any local clubs, societies or charities. Just as a good school community relies on the people who are part of it, a successful local community depends on the attitudes of the people living and working within that community. Explain that some children have been interviewing people from the local community.

EXAMPLE: a police officer, a nurse, a councillor, a postal worker, etc.

Invite those children to come to the front and give a short talk, explaining the role in the community of the person that was interviewed. They may also wish to share some of the questions they asked and say how they chose these questions. They may also wish to show relevant photos and artefacts.

NOTE ☐ You may wish to allow some time for the children listening to ask questions.

Some children may also wish to talk about how they have become more involved in the local community, as part of their work in the classroom.

At this point, invite your guest speaker to the front. Let him/her spend a few minutes talking about the local charity which he/she represents. The speaker may be able to suggest ways in which the children can become involved in the charity.

NOTE ☐ You may already have raised some money for the charity at a school event, in which case it would be a good opportunity to present the speaker with a cheque.

Finish the assembly with the following reflection.

REFLECTION

Let us give thanks for our happy and supportive school community and the many people which make it work so well. Let us also think about our local community and about the people who work within it. Let us give thanks for the jobs they do and let us think about the ways in which we can be a useful part of it.

ADDITIONAL RESOURCES AND ACTIVITIES

> The older children could write and make their own books to share with younger classes.

> If it is not already being done, some of the older children can take on jobs such as helping to supervise the younger children at lunch-time.

> Encourage the children to become more involved in the local community.

  EXAMPLE: assist with some local voluntary work or join a local club or society.

> A free, informative colourful activity book, *Euroquest* for Key Stage 2 pupils contains a trail of questions and answers about the European Union, the group of European nations held together by common traditions, political and economic interests.
  Contact your local European Resource Centre for Schools and Colleges for information.

  • Visit the European Union website:
    http://wwwcec.org.uk/info/pubs/catalog.htm.

> There are many examples of children trying to help or save their community. The African Children's Choir was formed in the 1980's, and made up of children from areas where there was poverty, hunger and war. They now tour the world raising awareness and money for their communities.

> Many people have to leave their community and seek refuge in other countries. The children could research the major refugee movements of the 20th century and track these on a map.

> The children could find out about matters of interest in their local community - famous people who live or have lived there, historic incidents or festivals that take place now or used to take place there. They could also find out about facilities that are available for the community - library, community centre, sports centres, health clubs, parks and playgrounds.

SPRING TERM

MY FEELINGS

1. MY NEW YEAR RESOLUTION

> PSHE LINK: FEELING POSITIVE ABOUT THEMSELVES
> SETTING PERSONAL GOALS

RESOURCES AND ORGANISATION

You will need:-

- 1 Flip chart with a collection of pictures or photographs with Spring associations.

    EXAMPLE: Easter eggs, chicks, lambs, a maypole, blossom, daffodils, etc.

- Objects which are reminiscent of Spring.

    EXAMPLE: an egg, a green plant showing new shoots or buds, a packet of seeds, a feather duster for Spring cleaning, etc.

- A set of 10 Resolution Cards with New Year Resolutions written on the front and a letter on the back of each which spell out the word SPRINGTIME.

- 10 preselected children who have written their own New Year Resolutions in class to hold up the Resolution Cards with their own Resolutions written on the fronts.*
        *or 10 children chosen on the day to read out the sample New Year Resolutions from the Resolution Cards.

WHAT TO DO

Start the assembly by asking the children if they had a good holiday/Christmas. Explain that we are starting the Spring Term of the school year and, although the coming months may still be cold and feel wintery, we are looking ahead to springtime.

QUESTION: What first comes into their heads when they think about Spring?

Show them the flip chart with its clues.

• QUESTION: What things do they associate with Spring?

Then show the various objects that are associated with Spring. Explain that Spring is often associated with new growth - plants are beginning to show green shoots and buds, many vegetables are sown, new lambs are born, and so on.

Although the beginning of our Spring Term at school is in January, and it is still very much winter, we are starting a new calendar year. Traditionally, this is a time when people make New Year Resolutions. This is when they make a promise to themselves that they are going to try to give up a bad habit, or try to do something positive or something which benefits others.

EXAMPLE: it could be anything from giving up chocolate to keeping their bedroom tidy.

Ask the children if any of them, or their parents, have made New Year Resolutions this year.

Continue by reading the following poem.

MY NEW YEAR'S RESOLUTIONS

I will not throw the cat out the window
Or put a frog in my sister's bed
I will not tie my brother's shoelaces together
Nor jump from the roof of Dad's shed
I shall remember my aunt's next birthday
And tidy my room once a week
I'll not moan at Mum's cooking (Ugh! Fish fingers again!)
Nor give her any more of my cheek.
I will not pick my nose if I can help it
I shall fold up my clothes, comb my hair,
I will say please and thank you (even when I don't mean it)
And never spit or shout or even swear.
I shall write each day in my diary
Try my hardest to be helpful at school
I shall help old ladies cross roads (even if they don't want to)
And when others are rude I'll stay cool.

I'll go to bed with the owls and be up with the larks
And close every door behind me.
I shall squeeze from the bottom of every toothpaste tube
And stay where trouble can't find me.
I shall start again, turn over a new leaf,
Leave my bad old ways forever
Shall I start them this year, or next year
 Shall I sometime, Or . . . . . ?

Robert Fisher

My New Year's Resolutions © Robert Fisher
from Let's Celebrate - Festival Poems, by John Foster
Oxford University Press.

Invite each of the preselected children in turn to read out their
own New Year Resolution written on the back of one of the
ten cards spelling the word SPRINGTIME.

NOTE ☐ Alternatively you may wish to use the Sample
Resolution Cards, with each resolution beginning
with one of the letters of the word springtime, and
invite a group of children to read these out.

SAMPLE RESOLUTION CARDS

RESOLUTION CARDS
S

Spend more time on my homework.

RESOLUTION CARDS

P

Put the lid on the toothpaste tube.

RESOLUTION CARDS

R

Remember to clean out my hamster's cage.

RESOLUTION CARDS

I

I will tidy my room once a week.

RESOLUTION CARDS

N

Not spend as much time watching television.

RESOLUTION CARDS

G

Go to bed earlier and get up earlier on weekdays.

RESOLUTION CARDS

T

Try my hardest to be helpful at school.

RESOLUTION CARDS

I

I will not forget to say please and thank you.

RESOLUTION CARDS

M

My pocket money will not go on sweets and crisps.

```
RESOLUTION CARDS

                    E
```

```
Every day I will write a new entry in my diary.
```

Finish the assembly with the following reflection.

REFLECTION

Let us give thanks for our recent holidays and think for a moment about our own special New Year's Resolutions, whether they are things we are going to do at home or at school.

ADDITIONAL RESOURCES AND ACTIVITIES

> The children could use the internet to research festivals and traditions which take place, or are connected with Spring. How was the coming of springtime celebrated in this country in the past? How is spring cleaning connected with the Jewish Passover?

> The children could make seasonal collages and pictures.

> The children could write New Year Resolution poems.

> The children could make up 'impossible resolutions'.

> The children could design a New Year Resolution Contract with a section both for school and at home. You could link the New Year Resolution Contract to setting personal goals.

> January is named after the Roman god, Janus, the patron of the beginning of the day, month and year. He is represented in art with two faces looking in opposite directions. The children could find out about him.

2. I'M FEELING GOOD

PSHE LINK: FEELING POSITIVE
RECOGNISING THEIRS AND OTHERS' WORTH
AS INDIVIDUALS

RESOURCES AND ORGANISATION

You will need:-

- 1 large foam or other soft ball.

- A group of preselected children to present some rehearsed freeze-frames showing a selection of emotions.

- A second group of preselected children to read out class work short pieces of writing on why they like a particular friend and then to play **The Compliment Game**.

WHAT TO DO

> Start the assembly by inviting the group of children up to present the freeze-frames.

Then play some light, cheerful music.

EXAMPLE: *'Don't Worry Be Happy'* by Bobby McFerrin.

Every so often stop the music so that one selected child from the group can make a frozen statue showing a particular emotion.

EXAMPLE: sadness, anger, happiness, fear, envy, anxiety, pride.

Each time the music stops ask the children watching if they can tell, by looking at the child's body language, how each child is feeling.

Explain that often you can tell how someone is feeling just by looking at the expression on their face or their body language.

Invite the freeze-frame children back up to strike their poses again. Explain the situation behind each freeze-frame and ask the children watching to suggest something that you could do or say, as a friend, in each situation.

NOTE ☐ You might prefer to use your own situations in place of the suggested situations.

SUGGESTED SITUATIONS

sadness • Jenny's pet cat has just died.

• QUESTION: What could you do or say to make her feel better?

anger • Sam has just lost in an important football match.

• QUESTION: How could you calm him down?

happiness • Nita has just found out that her parents are taking her to Florida for her summer holiday.

• QUESTION: What do you say to her?

fear • Gill is frightened of spiders and is rigid with fear as a huge spider walks up her arm.

• QUESTION: What could you do and say?

envy • Colin has just seen his best friend boasting about his expensive birthday present of a bike. His bike is old and getting too small for him and he can't afford a new one.

• QUESTION: What could they both do?

anxiety • Helen is new in school and standing alone in the playground with no one to play with.

• QUESTION: What could you do to help?

pride • Jack has just won a colouring competition.

• QUESTION: How could you compliment him on his achievement?

Explain that part of being a good friend is trying to understand how the other person is feeling. Sometimes it is not easy to work out what is the best thing to do or say to make a friend feel better, but often just being there is enough. Friendships are important and we choose our friends for all sorts of different reasons. Often we choose friends for their different qualities.

At this point, invite the children to come up and read pieces they have written about their friends. Each piece should be a short description of the friend and a list of the qualities that the child sees and likes in that particular friend.

EXAMPLE: My friend is kind, reliable, friendly, generous, patient.

Continue by saying how important it is to compliment or praise people. Both giving and receiving compliments is a pleasant experience.

> Invite the second group of children to play the **Compliment Game.**

COMPLIMENT GAME

In this game the children stand in two rows facing each other and perpendicular to the audience. Give the ball to one child, who must throw it across to a child in the opposite row. The child who threw the ball must then compliment the other child in some way.

EXAMPLE: You tell good jokes, you are good at football, you smile a lot, etc.

The child receiving the ball and the compliment must then say, 'Thank you' and continue the process by passing the ball to someone else.

Ask the children playing the game what it felt like to give/receive compliments. Ask the children watching why we need to praise and compliment people.

• QUESTION: What would it be like if we never received or gave any praise?

• QUESTION: Does everybody deserve praise?

Finish with the following reflection.

REFLECTION

Help us to recognise and praise the good things about other people. Also help us to recognise our own talents and good qualities and to feel positive about ourselves. It is very easy to pick faults and criticise but people often respond better when they are praised and their good points are valued.

ADDITIONAL RESOURCES AND ACTIVITIES

> In drama individuals or small groups of children could form tableaux using body language to express feelings and the others could try to guess. *Drama•Dance•Singing Teacher Resource Book*, edited by John Nicholas, Dramatic Lines, provides useful ideas for non-verbal communication activities.

> In drama the children could act out short scenes where a problem or worry is resolved.

> The children could think about the ways in which animals show how they are feeling.

    EXAMPLE: a dog wagging it's tail, a cat purring.

> In art children could study pictures and sculptures which show emotion and feeling, and think about how the artist was able to portray feeling.

    EXAMPLE: the painting *The Scream*, Edvard Munch, 1893.
             the bronze *The Thinker*, Auguste Rodin, 1879-89.

> In PSHE the children could think about the kinds of things that worry them and try to find ways to resolve or deal with these anxieties.

> A useful teacher resource, which uses fairy tales to deal with conflict resolution is *Once upon a Conflict* by Tom Leimdorfer, Communication and Fund-raising Department of the Religious Society of Friends, on behalf of Quaker Peace and Service and Pax Christi. ISBN 0901689386
Tel: 0208 203 4884.

> An invaluable teacher resource is *Parables for Little People* by Lawrence Castagnola, Resource Publications, Inc. These wonderful, imaginative tales provide a prefect way to work on dealing with feelings and emotions. *Chore's Magic* and *The Frog Princess* are two appropriate stories to use here.

> Read the children the fable *The Jackdaw and the Pigeon,* * Aesop - the Complete Fables, Penguin.
>> *Moral - be content with what you've got.

> Discuss with the children the hopes that they have for their own future and their hopes for mankind.

> Discuss special times when we may feel positive. e.g. New Year at school (Hoping to do better). New Year (Making Resolutions). Starting a new job (Making a success of it). Birthdays, etc.

> Discuss why the snowdrop and the star are thought of as signs of hope.

> Read the Greek myth about Pandora's Box. The children could then design and make their own box to include the "sprite of hope".

3. SETTING GOALS
AND CELEBRATING ACHIEVEMENTS

PSHE LINK: FEELING POSITIVE
SETTING PERSONAL GOALS
RECOGNISING THEIR WORTH AS INDIVIDUALS

RESOURCES AND ORGANISATION

You will need:-

- 4 Colourful Target Cards with target, goal and achievement headings written on them.

- 8 White Statement Cards.*
            *with children's statements written in class
                or the Sample Statements used instead.

- Preselected children to share the work they have done in class during PSHE with their teacher, recognising achievements, setting goals and targets, or outlining the things they would like to improve or strengthen which have been written on the white Statement Cards.

    EXAMPLE: I want to be in the school swimming team.

- 4 Children to hold up the colourful Target Cards.

- A group of preselected children to present rehearsed tableaux and mimes celebrating their own achievements.

WHAT TO DO

Start the assembly by asking the children to put up their hands if they know what they are going to do after school.

- QUESTION: Do they know what they are going to do in the next summer holidays?

- QUESTION: Do they know which subjects they are going to choose to study at secondary school?

- QUESTION: Have they decided what career they would like when they are older?

Explain that in today's assembly they will be thinking about setting goals and celebrating achievements. Deciding what job they want to do when they are older is probably something they haven't given much thought to, but they may have thought about the things they would like to achieve in the much nearer future.

Sometimes it is useful to look at our lives, assessing our strengths and weaknesses, and decide what we would like to achieve in the future. In their class, they may have set goals or targets with their teacher, outlining the things they would like to improve or strengthen.

In many jobs people set themselves targets or goals to help them achieve what they want. Many successful and famous people have achieved their ambitions by setting themselves targets and persevering until they succeed.

Invite the first group of children up to share the PSHE work they have done in class. Four children can hold up the Target Cards.

COLOURFUL TARGET CARDS

TARGET CARDS

things I am proud of at school

TARGET CARDS

**school targets -
things I would like to improve or achieve**

```
┌─────────────────────────────────────────┐
│ TARGET CARDS                             │
│                                          │
│   things I am proud of outside school    │
│                                          │
└─────────────────────────────────────────┘
```

```
┌─────────────────────────────────────────┐
│ TARGET CARDS                             │
│                                          │
│            personal goals                │
│                                          │
└─────────────────────────────────────────┘
```

Then children from this group can read out what is written on the Statement Cards, one by one, and go to stand by the appropriate target, goal or achievement heading.

EXAMPLE: The child with a Statement Card that reads, I would like to improve my handwriting, goes to stand by the school targets card.

NOTE ☐ These targets and personal goals are likely to be very varied.

SAMPLE STATEMENT CARDS

```
┌─────────────────────────────────────────┐
│ STATEMENT CARDS                          │
│                                          │
│   I would like to improve my handwriting.│
│                                          │
└─────────────────────────────────────────┘
```

```
┌─────────────────────────────────────────┐
│ STATEMENT CARDS                          │
│                                          │
│             I listen well.               │
│                                          │
└─────────────────────────────────────────┘
```

```
┌─────────────────────────────────────────┐
│ STATEMENT CARDS                          │
│                                          │
│           I always do my best.           │
│                                          │
└─────────────────────────────────────────┘
```

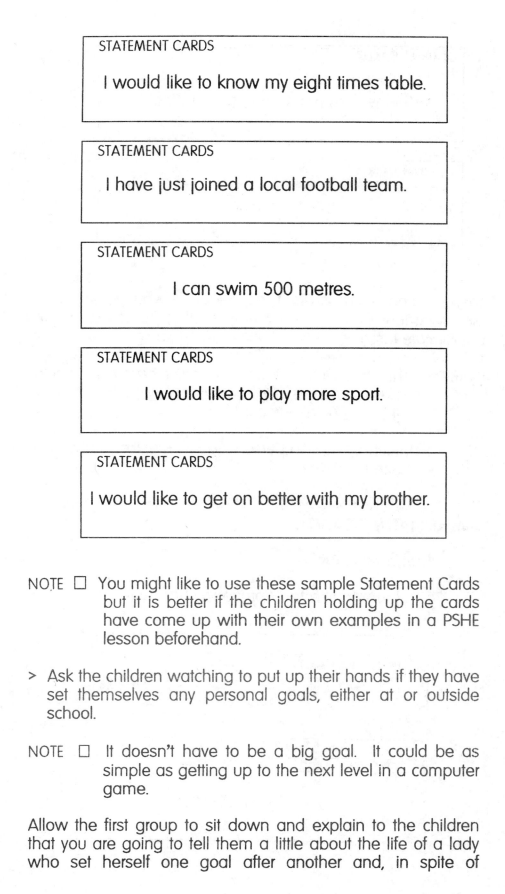

STATEMENT CARDS

I would like to know my eight times table.

STATEMENT CARDS

I have just joined a local football team.

STATEMENT CARDS

I can swim 500 metres.

STATEMENT CARDS

I would like to play more sport.

STATEMENT CARDS

I would like to get on better with my brother.

NOTE ☐ You might like to use these sample Statement Cards but it is better if the children holding up the cards have come up with their own examples in a PSHE lesson beforehand.

> Ask the children watching to put up their hands if they have set themselves any personal goals, either at or outside school.

NOTE ☐ It doesn't have to be a big goal. It could be as simple as getting up to the next level in a computer game.

Allow the first group to sit down and explain to the children that you are going to tell them a little about the life of a lady who set herself one goal after another and, in spite of setbacks and struggles, achieved some amazing things. Her name was Helen Keller.

HELEN KELLER

Helen Keller was born in Alabama, in the USA, on 27th June 1880. She was born a healthy baby and by the time she was nineteen months old she could walk, say a few words and was a happy and friendly toddler. However, this was soon to change. She caught a terrible fever and, although she survived, it left her unable to see or hear. It was as if she had been thrown into some kind of dark prison, from which there was no escape. As a young child it must have been very frightening, as she had no idea why her life had suddenly changed in this way.

Helen was an intelligent child and had a very determined character. As she grew older she began to use her other senses to explore the world around her. She would follow her mother around the house, hanging onto her skirts. She would touch and smell everything she came across, feeling people's hands to see what they were doing as she tried to make sense of the world. By copying other people's actions she was able to do simple jobs around the house and garden. She invented signs with her hands, in order to communicate with her family. By the age of seven she had invented sixty different signs. In this way she was able to communicate simply and understand something of the confusing world around her.

Although Helen was intelligent and determined, as she got older she realised how different she was from other children and this made her angry and frustrated. She would have terrible tantrums, she would kick and scream and at the dinner table she would snatch other people's food from their plates or throw objects onto the floor. Her family found it increasingly difficult to know how to deal with her.

Just before Helen's seventh birthday her family hired a private tutor called Anne Sullivan. Anne, blind as a child herself, and growing up in a poor home had not had an easy life. She had, however been lucky enough to get a place at the Perkins School for the Blind in Boston. Here she quickly earned herself a reputation for rudeness and bad behaviour, but after two successful eye operations was able to see properly and eventually left the college, graduating with honours. She seemed like a good choice for teaching Helen and, through her own hard work and determination, succeeded in transforming Helen's life.

Anne understood why Helen was behaving so terribly and realised that there was a very different girl underneath her angry exterior. She taught Helen the manual alphabet and, later, to write in Braille. She also taught Helen to speak by holding her fingertips against people's lips and feeling the vibrations and movements. Helen was eager to learn, although Anne had many battles whilst trying to teach the stubborn and frustrated Helen. Anne would let Helen touch an object and then spell the name onto her hand.

One day she poured water from the water pump onto Helen's hand, spelling out the letters W A T E R. As she did this, again and again, Helen suddenly realised, with excitement, what the signs represented. As soon as she realised this, she was desperate to learn. She understood that everything had a name and she wanted to know words for everything around her.

Anne continued to teach Helen, concentrating on those subjects which really interested her. As Helen grew older Anne continued to teach her, first at the Perkins Institute for the Blind and then at Wright-Humason School for the Deaf in New York where Anne attended the lessons with Helen, acting as her interpreter. Helen worked hard and proved that she had an excellent memory.

In 1904 she graduated from Radcliffe College with honours, having also published her life story, earning her enough to buy her own house. She went on to set up the American Foundation for the Blind in order to improve services to people with impaired vision. She also toured the country, giving lectures and becoming more and more famous. Her teacher, Anne Sullivan, accompanied her everywhere for almost fifty years.

Kryssy Hurley

Helen Keller proved herself to be a very remarkable woman and showed the world that disability is not a barrier to success. It is inspiring to see how much she achieved, in spite of the obstacles in her way, and shows us what can be achieved with determination and perseverance.

At this point, invite the group of children up to perform mimes and tableaux displaying a selection of skills and achievements.

NOTE ☐   The mimes/tableaux can show any skill or activity that these children are proud of, whether at school or in their leisure time.

EXAMPLE: a sporting activity, dancing, skateboarding, playing a musical instrument, etc.

Some children may also wish to show certificates, cups or badges that they are proud to have gained.

> Finish by applauding all the children who have taken part in the last activity.

Sum up by saying that everyone has some kind of skill or talent which they can be proud of. More important than how many talents or achievements you have, is how you make the most of these talents. Everyone can be proud of their strengths and achievements, at the same time as setting themselves goals and trying to strengthen their weaknesses.

Finish the assembly with the following reflection.

REFLECTION

Let us celebrate our talents and be proud of our achievements. Help us to have the determination and courage to set ourselves goals, to be successful and to realise our dreams. Let us think for a moment about people like Helen Keller who are able to achieve great things because of hard work, determination and the help and support of others.

ADDITIONAL RESOURCES AND ACTIVITIES

> Useful books for follow up work on Helen Keller: *Helen Keller* by Dorothy Herzmann, University of Chicago Press. *The Story of my Life* by Helen Keller, Bantam Classics.

Helen Keller: Courage in the Dark by Johanna Hurwitz and Neverne Covington, Random House.

> The children could find out about Braille.

> On the theme of perseverance look at the poem *Try Again* by E Cook, Book of a Thousand Poems, Evans.

> The children could collect accounts of brave deeds and achievements in the press.

> The children could read the story of Captain Oates on Scott's expedition to the Antarctic.

> The children could read the story of Robert the Bruce.

> Relate the assembly to PSHE work in class, fill in Record of Achievement and Self-assessment sheets with the children.

> The children could put together a classroom display board celebrating their achievements.

> You could find out about the lives of saints and martyrs:
  a) For the comprehensive Catholic account of any saint, see the Catholic Encyclopedia.

  • Visit the website: **www.newadvent.org/cathen/**

  b) A selective series of biographies is provided by the Catholic Information Network.

  • Visit the website: **www.cin.org/saints**

  c) For the Anglican Church's calendar.

  • Visit the website:
    www.cofe.epinet.co.uk/commonship/calendar/calendarfront

  d) Information on Orthodox saints is available from:
    St George Orthodox Information Service,
    The White House, Mettingham, Bungay, Suffolk NR35 1TP.

  e) For resources on Orthodox saints Key Stages 3 and 4.

  • Visit the website: **www.antiochian-orthodox.co.uk**

4. RELATIONSHIPS AND RESPECT

> PSHE LINK: DEVELOP GOOD RELATIONSHIPS

RESOURCES AND ORGANISATION

You will need:-

- A set of 13 Relationship Cards with a letter of the word RELATIONSHIPS written in large capitals on the front of each.

- 1 Flip chart for the relationship situation activity.

- 1 large card model of a set of traffic lights.*
  *or a set of traffic lights drawn on a sheet on the flip chart.

- 13 Preselected children who have worked in class on selecting a list of qualities which are important in a relationship written on the backs of the Relationship Cards.

  NOTE ☐ Alternatively 13 children can be chosen on the day to hold up the Sample Relationship Cards.

WHAT TO DO

Start the assembly by saying that we are going to be thinking about relationships.

> Ask the children to put up their hands if they think good relationships are easy to maintain.

Of course, this is not true. All relationships have ups and downs. Sometimes we fall out with or disagree with our friends. If it is a good relationship, then hopefully it will survive these ups and downs.

Explain that some children are going to hold up cards and call out some of the qualities that they think are important in a good relationship.

SAMPLE RELATIONSHIP CARDS

RELATIONSHIP CARDS

R

Reliable

RELATIONSHIP CARDS

E

Easy going

RELATIONSHIP CARDS

L

Likeable

RELATIONSHIP CARDS

A

An honest person

RELATIONSHIP CARDS

T

Trustworthy

RELATIONSHIP CARDS

I

Interesting

RELATIONSHIP CARDS

O

Listens to my Opinion

RELATIONSHIP CARDS

N

Nice to be with

RELATIONSHIP CARDS

S

RELATIONSHIP CARDS

Shares things with me

RELATIONSHIP CARDS

H

RELATIONSHIP CARDS

Has respect for me

RELATIONSHIP CARDS

I

RELATIONSHIP CARDS

I like the same things that they do

RELATIONSHIP CARDS

P

RELATIONSHIP CARDS

Patient

```
┌─────────────────────────────────────┐
│ RELATIONSHIP CARDS                   │
│                                      │
│                 S                    │
│                                      │
└─────────────────────────────────────┘
┌─────────────────────────────────────┐
│                                      │
│              Sensitive               │
│                                      │
│                                      │
└─────────────────────────────────────┘
```

NOTE ☐ It might be necessary to use these sample qualities but It is better if the children holding the cards up have thought up their own examples in a lesson beforehand.

Continue by saying that we are going to look at some situations which might happen in a relationship and you would like the children to try to think of a way of resolving the situation.

SITUATION ONE

Jenny and Claire live next door to each other. They are best friends and they have known each other for a long time. Every day they walk to school together and at play time they play together. A new girl, Mary, has just joined the school and Claire has become friends with her. Claire is a really good swimmer and Mary swims at the same club, so they have a lot to talk about. Jenny is feeling a bit left out and is worried that Claire has found a new friend.

- QUESTION: What could each of the girls do to make the situation easier.

EXAMPLE: Jenny could explain to Claire how she feels, Claire could play with both her friends at playtime and Jenny could try to make some new friends as well.

- QUESTION: Are there any qualities which the girls need to show.

EXAMPLE: patience, understanding.

SITUATION TWO

John and Bill are friends. Bill is always bringing expensive and new toys to school to play with. John hardly has any new toys because his parents can't afford them. Bill is always happy to share his toys with John but he does boast a lot about how much they cost. John feels embarrassed that he doesn't have any new toys. This also makes him angry and he tells Bill that he doesn't want to play with him.

- QUESTION: What could each of the boys do to make the situation easier?

Go on to ask if there are any qualities which the boys need to show.

EXAMPLE: sensitivity.

SITUATION THREE

Andy lives with his parents and his grandfather. His grandfather is very ill and his parents are busy looking after him, so they don't have much time to give to Andy. Andy is worried about his grandfather and he is also feeling that his parents aren't giving him much attention. At school he is always in a bad mood and he is getting into lots of arguments. His friends are beginning to get fed up with him.

- QUESTION: What could his best friend, Pete, do to help get things better?

- QUESTION: Are there any qualities which Pete or Andy need to have?

EXAMPLE: They both need to listen to each other's view.

NOTE ☐ List all the qualities on the flip chart as they emerge from discussion of each of the three situations.

Then ask the children to look at, and reflect upon, the qualities which you have written on the flip chart. Ask them to think about whether they have those qualities and whether there are any qualities they need to develop.

A good way for us to think about how we are showing these qualities is to imagine a set of traffic lights.

> Hold up the cardboard model of a set of traffic lights.

Explain that all the qualities and attitudes that we find easy go in the green circle, those which need to be developed a little go in amber and really hard to develop ones go in red.

TRAFFIC LIGHTS EXAMPLE

GREEN • If you are *always* easy going and honest you would put those qualities in the **green circle**.

AMBER • If you are *usually* patient, then that would go in the **amber circle**, along with other qualities which you need to develop a little.

RED • The **red circle** is for those qualities you find *really hard* to develop. You might find it hard to be a good listener.

I'm sure most of us can think of qualities we have which would go in each of these three circles. Relationships don't always run smoothly and good friendships depend on both people working hard to make the relationship work.

Finish the assembly with the following reflection.

REFLECTION

Think about the set of traffic lights and try to think about which qualities you find come easily to you and which qualities you need to make an effort to develop a bit more. Which qualities do you look for in your friends and which qualities would your friends say you had if they had to describe you?

ADDITIONAL RESOURCES AND ACTIVITIES

> The children could fill in their own personal traffic light sheets and try to work on the qualities that they find hard to develop.

> The children could put together a wall display on Relationships and Friendship, perhaps with pictures of the qualities they think are important. They could also include photographs of things they like doing with their friends and family.

> In drama groups of children could role play some of the situations which arise in friendships. Each group could present a tableau of a situation for another group to try to interpret.

> Groups or pairs of children could be given relationship situations to write happy endings, or alternate endings for.

> Children could make up their own friendship rules, or friendship 'do's and don'ts' and display them or present them to the rest of the class.

> Read the fable *The Eagle and the Fox* * Aesop, The Complete Fables, Penguin.
> > *Moral - it is not wise to betray a friend.

> The children could think about acceptable behaviour in different contexts.

> EXAMPLE:

> > I can read: in school, in bed, sitting on a chair, on the bus.
> > I cannot read: while swimming, on a playground slide, climbing a tree.
> > I can shout: in the playground, at a football match, in the garden.
> > I cannot shout: in assembly, in the classroom, in the cinema.

> Discuss different types of relationships the children have. e.g. with adults, brothers and sisters, older people, parents and friends.

> Further reading for children: *Big Sister, Little brother*, T. Berger, Macdonald. *The Trouble With Jack*, S. Hughes, Bodley Head. *All About Simon and His Grandmother*, E. Roberts, Methuen. *People Around Us: Friends*, Black.

5. THE WAY I FEEL

> PSHE LINK: UNDERSTANDING THEIR OWN FEELINGS
> AND HOW THEIR ACTIONS
> AFFECT THEMSELVES AND OTHERS

RESOURCES AND ORGANISATION

You will need:-

- Preselected children to hold up pictures with captions that they have drawn in class to illustrate a selection of expressions which are to do with moods and feelings.

- 1 Flip chart.

- A group of preselected children to present examples of mood expressed through dance, music and art that they have put together in previous class sessions. Also to read out short sentences written in class on what makes them feel a certain way..

WHAT TO DO

Start the assembly by inviting the children up to present their pictures and captions. Explain that these pictures illustrate expressions which are to do with feelings.

EXAMPLE: 'see red', 'green with envy', 'down in the dumps', 'over the moon', 'in the pink', 'feeling blue'.

Ask the children watching if they can see what all the pictures have in common.

NOTE ☐ Someone should suggest that they are all to do with feelings.

Go on to say that we all experience different moods and feelings at different times. Sometimes we don't even know why we are feeling a certain way. Life would be very boring if we always felt the same. Sometimes we have to control our feelings, but it would not be a good idea to bottle up or hide our feelings all the time.

Ask the children watching to think of as many different feelings as they can.

NOTE □ Make a note of these feelings on the flip chart.

Explain that a group of children have been thinking about their feelings and have been composing music and creating pictures and dance sequences to express certain emotions and feelings. Invite the group up and introduce them to the children watching.

NOTE □ The children can use percussion instruments to create their own mood pieces. Small groups can compose their own dance/movement pieces to appropriate music, each expressing a particular feeling. They can also use paint and collage to represent emotions.

Ask the children watching to see if they can identify each feeling that the groups are trying to portray.

SUGGESTED FEELINGS

- anger
- excitement
- joy
- calm
- sadness
- envy
- happiness
- fear

The same group of children can go on to read some short sentences about what makes them feel a certain way.

EXAMPLE: 'I feel angry when my brother breaks my toys.'
'I feel excited when it's my birthday.' etc.

At this point you may wish to ask the children watching to give some examples of when and why they feel a certain emotion.

Finish the assembly with the following reflection.

REFLECTION

Let us think about all the different feelings we experience. Help us to control those feelings when they are hurting or upsetting someone else. Also, help us to try to understand why we are feeling the way we do and to use our feelings in a positive way.

ADDITIONAL RESOURCES AND ACTIVITIES

> In drama children could create tableaux to show different emotions. They could also use role play to explore different ways of dealing with certain negative feelings.

> The children could design a CD cover for one of the CDs listened to in class which covered a wide range of moods.

MUSIC SUGGESTIONS:

MOODS

- *The Millennium Show*, Peter Gabriel.
- *Play*, Moby.
- *Colours In the Wind*, from the film Pocahontas.
- *Sea Interludes from Peter Grimes*, Op.33, Benjamin Britten.
- *La Mer: three symphonic sketches*, Claude Debussy.
- *Overture: The Hebrides*, Op 26, Felix Mendelssohn
- *Concierto d'Aranjuez*, Joaquín Rodrigo.

HAPPY/JOYFUL

- *Water Music*, George Frederic Handel.
- *In the Summer time*, Mungo Jerry.
- *Country Dance*, Wolfgang Amadeus Mozart, *The Essential Mozart*, Decca.
- *African Mamba*, Supernatural, Santana.
- *El Salón México*, Aaron Copland.

SAD/HAUNTING/PEACEFUL

- *Frozen*, Ray of Light, Madonna.
- *Neptune*, The Planet's Suite, Op 32, Gustav Holst.
- *Lacrymosa*, the Requiem, Wolfgang Amadeus Mozart.
- *The Great Gig in the Sky*, Dark Side of the Moon, Pink Floyd.
- *Holding Back the Years*, Picture Book, Simply Red.

SINISTER/FRIGHTENING

- *Mars*, The Planets Suite, Op. 32, Gustav Holst.
- *On the Run*, Dark Side of the Moon, Pink Floyd.
- *Jaws*, theme music for the film, John Williams.
- *Night on Bare Mountain*, Modest Mussorgsky.
- *Dance Macabre*, Op 40, Camille Saint-Saëns.

AMUSING

- *Flight of the Bumble Bee*, Nicolai Rimsky-Korsakov.
- *Concerto for Double Bassoon*, Antonio Vivaldi, Bassoon Concertos, Centaur.

> The children could write lists of occasions when they feel frightened, angry, happy or sad. They might also think about how they might enjoy some of these uncomfortable feelings. e.g. a frightening roller-coaster ride or a ride on a ghost train.

> Discuss how it is important to tell people how you feel. How it is alright to cry. How it is important to try to feel positive. How it is important to know yourself.

> Ask the children if we can "measure" our feelings. Can we give marks out of ten for: a sense of humour, consideration towards others, kindness or helpfulness.

> Further reading for children. *I Was So Mad I Could Have Spit Book*, G. Frisen & P. Ekholm, Black. *The Happy Owls*, C. Piatti, Benn. *Miserable Aunt Bertha*, J. V. Lord & F. Maschler, Cape. *Albin Is Never Afraid*, U. Lofgren, Macdonald. *The Owl Who Was Afraid of the Dark*, J. Tomlinson, Methuen/Puffin. *What Are You Scared Of?* H. Larson, Black. *Where The Wild Things Are*, M. Sendak, Bodley Head.

6. IT MAKES ME ANGRY

PSHE LINK: UNDERSTANDING THEIR OWN FEELINGS
AND HOW THEIR ACTIONS AFFECT
THEMSELVES AND OTHERS

RESOURCES AND ORGANISATION

You will need:-

- Preselected children to read out anger poems they have written in class.

- A group of preselected children to tell the Story of Prince Llewellyn using shadow puppets or mime.*

*This is optional.

WHAT TO DO

> Start the assembly by asking the children to put up their hands if they ever get angry.

- QUESTION: What makes them angry?

- QUESTION: How do they feel when they are angry?

- QUESTION: What happens to you when you are angry?

- QUESTION: How does your body show anger?

- QUESTION: How do people react to you when you are angry?

- QUESTION: Is it always wrong to be angry or are there times when it is justified?

- QUESTION: Have they ever lost their temper and then regretted it?

angry troubled, feeling or showing extreme resentful, revengeful or passionate displeasure.

Explain that you are going to tell them a story about a man who was angry and you would like them to think about the consequences of his anger.

NOTE ☐ You can simply read the following story or you may wish to get some rehearsed children to perform it using shadow puppets or to act it out.

THE STORY OF PRINCE LLEWELLYN

A long time ago, in Wales, there lived a prince called Llewellyn. He loved to hunt and he owned a splendid pack of hunting hounds. Life was very different in those days. It was much tougher and people had to hunt animals for food. The hunting hounds would help Prince Llewellyn with the hunting but they would also protect him from the wild wolves which roamed the dark forests, also looking for food.

Llewellyn was proud of his pack of hounds for they were fine animals and they served him well. His favourite hound was called Gelert and was a faithful old dog who had been with the family for many years. Gelert was very fond of his master and Llewellyn treated him well.

Llewellyn also had a baby son who meant the world to him. When he left his home to go hunting he would leave his faithful dog, Gelert, to guard his baby son. He knew that Gelert would protect his son if a wolf happened to find it's way into his home. This way he was able to go off hunting and leave his son, without worrying about him. Gelert would sit patiently by the child's cradle, ever alert and watching for danger.

One day Llewellyn left on a hunting trip, as he normally would, kissing his son goodbye and leaving him with Gelert. However, not long after he had gone, a wild and vicious wolf found its way into Llewellyn's home. Llewellyn's son lay sleeping peacefully in his cradle, on a soft lamb skin rug.

Gelert jumped up with a start. He sensed something was not right. There was strange scent in the house. Gelert knew there was an intruder and he sensed that Llewellyn's baby son was in danger. He got up slowly and started to pad towards the door. Before he reached it, a huge wolf came running into the room and headed towards the baby's cradle.

Just as it was about to pounce on Llewellyn's son Gelert intercepted, trying to sink his teeth into the wolf's throat. But the wolf was strong and he fought back, ferociously. The two animals struggled against each other for some time. Both animals were badly wounded and there was blood everywhere.

The baby's cradle had been overturned during the fight and he lay underneath it, still asleep and unaware of what was happening around him. Finally, and after receiving many wounds himself, Gelert sank his sharp teeth again into the wolf's throat, this time killing him. The wolf lay dead, next to the baby's cradle, as Gelert fell to the ground in exhaustion, licking his wounds.

All at once Gelert heard the familiar sound in the distance of his master coming in through the great door. He got up and made his way towards him. Llewellyn entered his son's room. With horror, he saw the upturned cradle and Gelert covered in blood. His immediate thoughts were that Gelert had killed his baby son. Without hesitation, he drew his sword and plunged it into the dog, crying out in anger as he did so. Gelert, too weak to move, howled in pain as he collapsed to the ground. It was then that Llewellyn's child woke up and started crying. Llewellyn went over to the cradle and turned it over. As he did so he noticed the dead body of the wolf. Suddenly he realised that Gelert had saved his son's life and that, in a moment of anger, he had just killed his most faithful friend.

a Welsh legend retold by Kryssy Hurley

- QUESTION: How do you think Prince Llewellyn felt when he realised what he had done?

- QUESTION: How do you think the situation could have been prevented?

- QUESTION: What do you think the main message of this story is?

Continue the assembly by inviting children up to read out their poems about anger.

SUGGESTED TITLES

I See Red, I'm So Angry, Hopping Mad, It Makes Me Fume, Who Says I'm Angry? etc.

Finish the assembly by reading the following reflection.

REFLECTION

Help us to control our anger and to think before we say or do something which may hurt someone else. When we see or hear about things in the world which seem unjust or unfair help us to use our anger in a positive and constructive way.

ADDITIONAL RESOURCES AND ACTIVITIES

> In drama, the children could role play in situations which make them angry, experimenting to find out how anger can be controlled or a situation resolved.

> The children could write *'Anger Raps'* about how they calm themselves down when they get angry.

> The children could think about issues in the wider world which make them angry, and consider whether anger can be a positive thing sometimes. e.g. getting angry about issues such as pollution.

> You could read the children the story *Temper Temper* by Norman Silver, Hodder/Macdonald Young Books.

> The children could make a collection of "angry" words and phrases. e.g. seething with rage, blind fury, steamed up, losing your rag, bear with a sore head, furious, seeing red.

> Discuss facial expressions and see how body language can express anger. The children could mime and dance angrily.

> Discuss angry colours. e.g. red, orange, black and purple. The children could then paint angry patterns or figures.

> Find examples of religious leaders who have been angry encountering situations that they believe to be wrong.

7. GREED AND ENVY

PSHE LINK: UNDERSTANDING THEIR OWN FEELINGS
AND HOW THEIR ACTIONS AFFECT THEMSELVES
AND OTHERS

RESOURCES AND ORGANISATION

You will need:-

- A set of illustrations to go with the main story.*

  *This could be group work.

- 1 or more children chosen on the day to hold up the story illustrations.

- Preselected children to read out their own limericks and short pieces of writing.

WHAT TO DO

Start the assembly by asking the children if any of them have a birthday in the coming months.

- QUESTION: Have they thought about what they would like for their birthday?

- QUESTION: Have they ever seen something they want really badly in the shops but not been able to buy it?

- QUESTION: Have they ever wanted something someone else has?

- QUESTION: Have they ever got something and then wanted something even better?

Most of us can think of something we want. Some people want lots of things. Some people want things but are never satisfied with what they have. Some people don't enjoy what they have but are always envying what others around them have. Some people in the world don't have much at all.

Choose the child/children to hold up the illustrations. Explain that you are going to tell them a story about a boy who wanted something really badly.

JACK'S BIRTHDAY

It was the morning of Jack's birthday and he was opening his presents. He'd got most of the things he'd wanted - a new computer game, a football, some CDs - but he hadn't opened the present from his parents yet. He knew from the shape of it that it was a bicycle. He'd been going on at his parents for the last month about getting a bike. His old bike was much too small for him and most of his friends had new bikes.

His best friend, Sam, had just been bought the newest most expensive model in the big store down town. For the last few weeks he had been calling in at the store, on the way home from school, to admire the model. His parents knew how much he wanted it and it would be great if he and Sam had the same bikes. They could ride them to school together and all the other kids would be jealous.

> Put your hand up if you have ever wanted something really badly, like Jack wanted the bike.

'Go on, Jack. Open your main present,' urged his dad.

'I wonder what it could be!' said his mum smiling.

Tentatively he peeled back some of the wrapping paper. He was silently hoping and praying it was the bike he wanted. He peeled some more paper back.

'I know it's not the bike you had you're eye on,' his dad said, 'but we just couldn't afford it. I was going to look for a second hand bike but the guy in the shop said we can pay for this one in instalments so we thought we'd get you a new one.'

'The man said it was a very popular model,' his mum added.

• QUESTION: How do you think Jack feels?

- QUESTION: How do you think his parents feel?

Jack looked at the bike, trying to hide his disappointment. It was certainly a nice looking bike, but nothing compared to the bike he had wanted. It wasn't fair. It was the only thing he'd really wanted. Surely his parents could have afforded it. Sam's parents hadn't thought twice about buying it. It just wasn't fair.

He thanked his parents, although he was sure they could tell he wasn't very happy.

'Why don't you meet Sam and go for a ride now!' his dad suggested.

'No, it's OK. I'll go later. I think I'll just go for a walk.'

- QUESTION: How do you think Jack's parents are feeling now?

- QUESTION: Where do you think Jack is going?

Jack decided to head for town. He wanted to see if the bike was still in the store. Maybe he could persuade the manager to take the other bike back and he could arrange to pay for the bike bit by bit, every month. It would be worth waiting if he could have the best model in the store. When he got to the store he went straight to the bike section. It was gone. His beautiful bike had gone. He asked the sales assistant where the bike was.

'Sold the last one today,' she replied. 'They're lovely bikes, very well made. Expensive, though.'

Jack decided to have a look round the rest of the store while he was there. He still had a small amount of birthday money to spend. Maybe he'd get another game for his computer, or a model plane for his collection.

He made his way to the computer section and sat down next to a boy who was trying out one of the latest games.

'This is a fantastic game,' the boy said, excitedly, 'My dad's just said he'll buy it for me if I want. Here, have a go!'

Jack took over the controls. The boy was right. It was a good game.

'Hey, you're really good. Have you played it before?' the boy asked.

'Only a few of times. My best friend's got it and we sometimes we do swaps.'

'That's a good idea. Look, my dad has just said I can choose three games today. I know I want this one but I'm not sure which of the others to get. Any ideas?'

Jack quickly selected two more of his favourite games for the boy.

'I'd go for these, if you haven't already got them.' he said.

'Thanks, I will.'

'You're really lucky,' Jack went on, 'To have parents who will buy you what you want.'

'Yeah, they're pretty good to me. We're going on holiday next week and dad doesn't want me to be bored because . . . . . '

The boy's voice trailed off.

'I was after a bike,' Jack went on, 'A special bike. It was the one they had on the main display here. It was beautiful. But my parents said they couldn't afford it. It's a real pain.'

'I know the one you mean,' the boy replied. 'That was a real beauty. I noticed it when we came in last week.'

'Do you think your parent s might buy it for you?' Jack asked.

'Well, no. They can't you see, because . . . . . ' But before the boy could continue his dad approached and bent down to lift him out of his chair and into a wheelchair.

- QUESTION: What do you think Jack's reaction will be?

Jack realised at once that the boy couldn't walk, let alone ride a bike. He felt really stupid and embarrassed. The boy smiled pleasantly at him as his father pushed him away. Jack felt ashamed of himself. How greedy and selfish he'd been, envying Sam's bike. There he was, getting upset about not having the newest, most expensive bike in the store when there was someone would never be able to even ride a bike.

He jumped up and ran all the way home. There was something he had to do.

Kryssy Hurley

- QUESTION: What do you think Jack is going to do now and why do you think he ran home?

Continue by inviting a group of children to read out some work they have done in class on limericks about greedy or envious characters and short pieces of writing about things they have really wanted or people they have envied.

EXAMPLE LIMERICK

There was a young man from Kew
Who envied everyone he knew.
They all got to know,
Told him where to go,
And he found Hell less pleasant than Kew.

Finish the assembly by reading the following reflection.

REFLECTION

Let us think of people in the world who have a lot less than we do. There are always going to be people who have more than us and there are always going to be things which we want. But help us to appreciate and make the most of the things that we have.

ADDITIONAL RESOURCES AND ACTIVITIES

> The children could write, illustrate and act out their own fables and stories about people who are greedy or envious.

> You could read the children the story *Money Bags* from Parables For Little People by Lawrence Castagnolia, Resource Publications, Inc.

> The children could find out about living conditions in parts of the world where people do not have the things they want and where they often live without the things they need.

> The Buddhist religion teaches that it is only when we free ourselves from wanting things that we can reach the peace of Nirvana. This is why the Buddhist monks own only their begging bowls and have no worldly possessions to worry them. The children could find out how Buddhist monks live and about the philosophy behind Buddhism, possibly visiting a Buddhist temple or centre.

   For information on Buddhism of Nichiren Daishonin:
   SGI-UK, Taplow Court, Taplow, Maidenhead, Berkshire, SL6 OER. Tel: 01628 773163. Fax: 01628 773055

   • Visit the website: **www.sgi-uk.org**

> Read appropriate fables from Aesop - The Complete Fables, Penguin. *The Woman and the Hen* *
                                  * Moral - don't be greedy.
   The Goose with the Golden Eggs and *The Tortoise and the Eagle* are also appropriate.

> Further reading for children. The poem *Sometimes I Share Things* from Catch A Little Rhyme, Eve Merriam. The poem *One Sister For Sale* from The Poems and Drawings of Shel Silverstein. The story *The Greedy Cat and The Parrot*, S. C. Bryant, Methuen.

8. SELFISHNESS

PSHE LINK: UNDERSTANDING THEIR OWN FEELINGS
AND HOW THEIR ACTIONS AFFECT THEMSELVES
AND OTHERS

RESOURCES AND ORGANISATION

You will need:-

- A group (minimum 3 - 9 +) of preselected children to
rehearse and act out the story of the Selfish King.

THE SELFISH KING
CAST
(Speaking parts)
King
Queen
Servant

(Optional non-speaking parts)
General
Prisoner
Poor Mother
Young Boy
Prime Minister
Doctors

NOTE ☐ You may wish to also use a child to act as the
Narrator.*

*If you choose not to narrate.

WHAT TO DO

Ask the children if they can explain what the word selfish
means.

selfish 1. without consideration for others, too much concerned
with one's own personal welfare or interests and having little
or no concern for others, self-centred. 2. showing or prompted
by self-interest.

- QUESTION: Can they think of any examples where someone has acted selfishly?

- QUESTION: Can they remember having ever acted selfishly?

Tell them that some children are going to act out a story about an Italian king who acted out of selfishness.

THE SELFISH KING

NARRATOR: Long ago, in Italy, there lived a king and his queen. The king had come to own a very special green bottle. The bottle was quite small but it was believed that it contained the elixir of life.

KING: This bottle is very precious, my dear queen. It will cure any illness and it is said that the person who drinks it will live forever. I must keep it somewhere **very** safe.

QUEEN: That is indeed amazing, my king. We must keep it very safe.

NARRATOR: The king put the bottle in a glass cupboard near to his throne.
(LONG PAUSE. The Narrator moves forward.)
One day the queen came running to the king.

QUEEN: Come quickly, husband. One of your greatest generals is dying. Over the years he has **won** many battles for you and it is because of him our kingdom is safe. Let us give him a drop of liquid from the green bottle so that he may live to see his grandchildren.

KING: Oh, no. I can't do that, my dear. I'm saving the liquid in this bottle for something really special.

QUEEN: Very well, my dear. As you say.

NARRATOR: Shortly afterwards news came that the general had died.

(LONG PAUSE. The Narrator takes a few steps.)

Some time later, news came that one of the king's prisoners was dying. The man was not an evil man. He had been put in prison for stealing some food for his family. Now he was very ill and wanted to live to see his family and friends and to see the outside world again.

QUEEN: Come quickly, husband. We need your little green bottle. This man is about to die. Let me give him some of the liquid and set him free to see his family.

KING: You can't do that! I absolutely forbid it. I'm saving that liquid for someone who really needs it. I'm sorry, my dear, but my decision is final.

QUEEN: You know best, I suppose.

NARRATOR: And so the prisoner died without seeing his family.
(PAUSE. The Narrator takes a few more steps.)
Some months later a young boy was badly injured in an accident. His poor mother came to the king to beg him for a drop of the magical liquid. The king looked at the woman's sad face and he was certainly moved. But still he could not bear to part with any of the liquid.

KING: I'm sorry, but I can't part with any of the elixir.

QUEEN I wish you would change your mind, my dear.

NARRATOR: But the king didn't change his mind and the young boy died later that day. *(PAUSE.)* As time went by more sick and dying people pleaded with the king to part with a drop or two of his special liquid. *(Narrator shakes head solemnly. PAUSE.)* Sometime later the Prime Minister became very ill, but still the king refused to part with a single drop of the

125

refused to part with a single drop of the precious liquid. The people of his kingdom began to talk about the king's actions. They realised that the king was saving the elixir for himself. The Prime Minister died and the people mourned the loss of a great and worthy man. And still the elixir sat in the glass cupboard by the king's throne. *(PAUSE.)* Many years went by. People had given up asking the king for so much as a single drop of the elixir. The king became ill himself and though the doctors tried there was nothing more they could do to help the king. He was dying. *(PAUSE.)* As he lay in his bed he called a servant over.

KING: Servant! Fetch me the little green bottle from the glass cabinet, and be careful you don't drop it.

SERVANT: Yes, master.

NARRATOR: The servant handed him the bottle. The queen watched as he carefully pulled out the cork.

KING: *(Horrified.)* What! Empty! It can't be!

NARRATOR: To his horror, the king realised that the bottle was empty. All the liquid had evaporated. He had kept the liquid for so long that every drop had evaporated. The king held the bottle in his hands and looked sadly at the queen. Suddenly he realised how selfish he had been.

KING: I have been a selfish man. I could have helped many people. Instead I chose to keep the liquid all for myself.

NARRATOR: With that the king let out a short gasp and died.

                                            Kryssy Hurley

Ask the children how they think the king felt as he held the empty bottle.

- QUESTION: Are there people in the world who act as selfishly as this?

- QUESTION: How do you think he might have felt if he'd used the elixir to help other people?

Finish the assembly with the following reflection.

REFLECTION

Let us reflect for a moment on the actions of the king in the story we have just heard. What could he have done differently? How did his actions affect those around him? Help us to think of others before we act, rather than acting selfishly and without thought.

ADDITIONAL RESOURCES AND ACTIVITIES

> The children could write alternate endings for the story *The Selfish King*.

> Alternatively, in a drama session, the children could create and act out their own dramatised versions and endings for a story about a selfish king.

> You could read the children the story *The Selfish Giant* by Oscar Wilde. The children could then illustrate it and retell it in their own words.

> The musical play *The Selfish Giant* from Introducing Oscar by Veronica Bennetts, Dramatic Lines can be performed as a play or unstaged as a choral work with the lines spoken.

> Further reading for children: *The Bad-tempered Ladybird*, Eric Carle, Harcourt Brace. *Emma Quite Contrary*, G. Wolde & A. Winn, Hodder. *All About MyNaughty Little Sister*, D. Edwards, Methuen.

9. SADNESS AND LONELINESS

> PSHE LINK: UNDERSTANDING THEIR OWN FEELINGS
> AND HOW THEIR ACTIONS
> AFFECT THEMSELVES AND OTHERS

RESOURCES AND ORGANISATION

You will need:-

- Preselected children to hold up pictures of sad and happy faces they have made.

- A second group of preselected children to read out short pieces of writing with ideas of how to cheer up your friends that were written in class.

WHAT TO DO

> Start the assembly by asking the children to hold up pictures of happy and sad faces.

Ask the children watching to say what kind of things make people happy or sad.

- QUESTION: Why do they think some people get lonely?

- QUESTION: What could you do if you see that one of your friends is looking sad?

  Explain that you are going to tell them a story about a woman who was sad and lonely.

THE LONELY OLD WOMAN

Jenny and her friends, Paul, Sam and Joanne would always walk to school together. It wasn't very far. It only took them about ten minutes and they got a chance to have a good chat. They used to pass old Mrs Brian's house on the way, a run-down cottage with an overgrown garden and dark curtains at the window, which always seemed to be closed.

The children were a bit afraid of Mrs Brian. The few times they'd seen her she'd shouted at them; and some of the children at school said that she was a witch. Of course they knew this wasn't true but they were still a bit frightened of her.

- QUESTION: Do you think the children were right to be frightened of her?

One day Sam had thrown Jenny's ball over the old woman's fence and she'd crept in to get it back. The old woman had seen her and had come out of the house and down the path towards her. She'd grabbed the ball and then run as fast as her legs would carry her. And the next time she'd walked past, Mrs Brian had shouted out to her. Jenny was on her own and she didn't hang around to find out what she wanted.

Some of the kids at school would pick apples from the branches which overhung the footpath from the tree in her front garden. They said that she used to have a husband but one day he'd suddenly disappeared. Joanne said she'd probably poisoned him. Jenny knew that couldn't be true but the thought made her shiver. So when she was on her own she'd run past the house hoping old Mrs Brian wouldn't see her.

- QUESTION: How do you think Mrs Brian felt about children?

One day Jenny's mother had asked her to drop some leaflets through the letterboxes of houses in some of the streets near their house. Joanne had said she'd help her. They took opposite sides of the street and it wasn't long before they'd nearly finished. They only had one more street to do, and it was the one where Mrs Brian lived. They decided to do one side at a time, together.

The girls were a bit nervous about walking up Mrs Brian's path but they told themselves there was nothing to be frightened of. As they walked up the path, the front door opened. It was Mrs Robinson, Jenny's neighbour.

- QUESTION: What do you think is going to happen?

'Hello, girls. How are you? Have you come to visit Mrs Brian? She'll like that. She doesn't get many visitors, and she's not been feeling all that well lately. Come on in. You can have one of the home-made biscuits I've brought round.'

The girls looked at each other, wondering what to say, as Mrs Robinson ushered them in.

'I've got some visitors for you, Madge. I'll just make them a drink and fetch those biscuits and then I'll have to leave you.'

'Well, we only came . . . . . ' Jenny started to say but stopped as she noticed the smile on Mrs Brian's face. She was surprised to see her smiling. She'd never seen her smile before. And she didn't look half so frightening close up. And Mrs Robinson seemed to think she was all right.

'We'll just stay five minutes,' she whispered to Joanne.

- QUESTION: Would you have stayed if you were in Jenny's situation?

Well, the two girls ended up staying almost an hour. Mrs Brian was quite an interesting woman. Apparently her husband had died two years ago and that was when the garden got overgrown. She showed them pictures of how the garden used to be. It looked lovely. It even had a pond. She said that they could come and pick apples whenever they wanted.

Mrs Brian then showed them photos of her son and her grandchildren, who lived in Australia. The girl looked about the same age as Jenny and Joanne. She really seemed to miss them. They were the only family she had now.

Jenny began to realise how lonely she must be, stuck in that big old cottage. She only used a couple of the rooms, which is why she kept most of the curtains shut.

• QUESTION: How do you think the girls feel now?

At last the girls had to go, before Jenny's mum started to worry about them. But they promised that they would call in and see her again. When they left Mrs Brian she looked so happy and cheerful they were glad they'd stayed to talk to her.

• QUESTION: Why do you think Mrs Brian looks so happy?

After that the girls started to call in to see her once a week. Sometimes they would have a game of cards or look at photos her son sent from Australia. Jenny's dad even helped them to tidy up her garden and Jenny took lots of photos of it and sent them on her computer to Mrs Brian's granddaughter, Lucy. After that, Lucy often sent Jenny e-mails, which Jenny would read to Mrs Brian.

Jenny couldn't believe they'd ever been afraid of Mrs Brian. In fact, Mrs Brian had probably been more afraid of them, especially when she'd seen children taking her apples and running off. And the only reason Mrs Brian had shouted at them was because she'd been sad, lonely and a bit afraid of the children she saw, but knew nothing about.

Over the next few months Mrs Brian became a bit of a favourite with Jenny and her friends. And the following year, when Mrs Brian's granddaughter, Lucy, came to stay with her she found she had a lot of friends waiting for her.

Kryssy Hurley

• QUESTION: Is it always easy to tell if someone is feeling sad?

• QUESTION: Is it always easy to tell if someone is feeling lonely?

Go on to say that sometimes all of us feel sad or lonely. An important part of being a true friend is to support people and cheer them up when they are feeling down.

Continue by inviting children to read out the ideas they have for cheering up their friends when they are feeling down.

EXAMPLE: telling jokes, getting the friend to join in a game, inviting the friend round, and so on.

Finish the assembly with the following refection.

REFLECTION

Let us think of those people in the world who are feeling sad at this moment. Help us to cheer up our friends when they are feeling sad or lonely and try to understand other people's feelings.

ADDITIONAL RESOURCES AND ACTIVITIES

> You could talk about what they might do if they see someone in the playground who is on their own or looking lonely. What do they think of ideas such as a 'buddy bench' or a 'bus stop' where children can go if they are looking for someone to play with?

> The children could make a display of pictures of happy and sad faces, along with writing about things that make us happy or sad.

> The children could find out about or write about countries where people have suffered because of a natural disaster.

NOTE ☐ You might like to show the children recent or topical press pictures and copy of droughts, floods, mud slides or earthquakes.

> The children could make life-size papier mâché heads by laying paper pieces or sheets over inflated balloons and then painting happy or sad faces on them.

> The children could make a list of things that make them sad and then another list of things that they or someone else could do to change them. An 'impossible list' could also be made showing things that are difficult to change.

10. WE'RE WORKING TOGETHER

> PSHE LINK: DEVELOPING GOOD RELATIONSHIPS

RESOURCES AND ORGANISATION

You will need:-

- Preselected children to present a number of rehearsed short mimes individually and in small groups.

- 2 Groups of children chosen on the day to work on a group challenge to **Build-A-House** each.

- House building equipment for each group:
  4 chairs, 2 large bed sheets, sticky tape, sheets of coloured sugar paper, scissors, string and bean bags.

- 1 Flip chart with a large sheet of card cut up to make four Team Cards. Write one letter of the word TEAM on each of the cards before placing them blank side up on the chart.*
  > *If you use pre-written replies the Team Cards will be placed on the chart later.

- 4 Children to take the Team Cards off the flip chart.

WHAT TO DO

Start the assembly by explaining that a group of children are going to present some very short snippets of mime. Afterwards, you are going to ask them if they noticed anything about the things the children were doing.

SUGGESTED SHORT MIME ACTIVITIES

- playing a game of tennis
- folding up a large sheet
- playing a board game like snakes and ladders
- telling jokes
- tidying up toys from the floor

Invite each child up, one at a time, to mime an activity snippet on their own.

Ask the children watching what they noticed about each activity snippet.

Someone may suggest that each scene involved a child doing something on their own, and that it would have been better, or more sensible, for another person to have been involved.

Tell them that the scenes are going to be acted out again, but slightly differently. This time the same activities will be acted out in mime but two or more children will be involved in each activity.

Invite pairs and small groups of children to mime the activity snippets.

Ask the children watching what differences they noticed this time.

Someone may suggest that the activities were more suited to two or more children.

- It is not possible to play a game of tennis without someone to play against.

- It is easier to fold a sheet if you have someone to help.

- It is pointless playing a board game designed for two or more players on your own.

- It is not much fun telling jokes if you have no one to listen to them.

- It is quicker and more enjoyable to tidy up if you have someone to help.

Go on to say that there are times when it is better to do an activity with someone else. Sometimes it is more fun and it is often easier to do difficult jobs with someone to help. Explain that in today's assembly we are thinking about team work and co-operation.

> Ask the children to put up their hands if they have ever been set a group task in class.

● QUESTION: What kind of things are important if you are working in a group?

EXAMPLE: Listen to others, take turns to talk, etc.

● QUESTION: Who plays a sport as part of a team?

In any team it is important that you work together. Go on to say that you are going to choose two groups of four children to undertake a group challenge to build a house.

NOTE ☐ These groups can be preselected or even rehearsed.

You would like the rest of the children to watch how they work together.

BUILD-A-HOUSE ACTIVITY

> Choose two groups and ask them to sit in two different areas.

Each group is provided with the same basic building equipment. They will have exactly five minutes to make a house with the given equipment. The house must fit at least two children inside and be recognisable as a house. It is up to them how they work and they must decide between them what each of them is going to do.

> Start them off.

> After five minutes stop the children and ask them to sit down next to their house.

Ask the first group to explain how they went about their task.

● QUESTION: Did they choose a group leader?

● QUESTION: Did they allocate tasks to each member?

● QUESTION: How long did they spend discussing what they were going to do at the start?

- QUESTION: Did they have any problems?

- QUESTION: Do they think there was anything they could have done better?

> Look at their house.

- QUESTION: Can two children fit inside?

- QUESTION: Does it resemble a house?

Ask the children watching if they have any comments on the way this group of children worked together.

Now do the same for the second group.

Ask the children in the groups, and the children watching, what they have learnt about working together in a group.

- QUESTION: What is important when you are working together?

- QUESTION: Do they think these skills may be important in later life?

- QUESTION: How might these skills be useful?

Write four of the replies to these questions on the blank Team Cards attached to the flip chart.

NOTE ☐ If you choose to use the pre-written Sample Team Cards instead place these on the flip chart with the working together points side showing.

SAMPLE TEAM CARDS

| TEAM CARDS |
| listen to other people |

| T |

TEAM CARDS
don't be bossy

E

TEAM CARDS
don't upset other people by being rude

A

TEAM CARDS
share the work fairly

M

Finish by asking four children to take the Team Cards off the flip chart, turn them around and hold them up for everyone to see.

- QUESTION: Can the four rearrange the cards to make a word?

When they have arranged the cards to spell the word **TEAM** explain that these letters can stand for Together Everyone Achieves More, a reminder that if we work together, co-operatively, we can often get more done.

Finish the assembly with the following reflection.

REFLECTION

Help us to remember that when we are working with others we need to co-operate and work as a team. Let us think about the way we work with others.

- QUESTION: Do we listen to what others have to say?

- QUESTION: Do we give our own opinion in a sensitive way?

- QUESTION: Do we do our fair share of the work?

- QUESTION: Do we think about other people's feelings?

All these things are important if we are to work successfully with other people.

ADDITIONAL RESOURCES AND ACTIVITIES

> Children can undertake group tasks and challenges in class and then report back on how they felt they worked together.

> Children can find out about well known teams and partnerships.

  EXAMPLE: Manchester United football team,

> You could read the children the parable *Chore's Magic* from Parables For Little People by Lawrence Castagnola, Resource Publications, Inc.

  NOTE ☐ This is a good way in to explore how we can deal with people who aren't helpful and co-operative.

> You could read the children the fable *The Three Oxen and the Lion** Aesop - The Complete Fables, Penguin.
  *Moral - It is safer to stay together.

> A useful resource for a wide variety of team games is *Aaargh to Zizz 135 Drama Games*, Graeme K. Talboys, Dramatic Lines.

11. SHARING AND GENEROSITY

PSHE LINK: DEVELOPING GOOD RELATIONSHIPS

RESOURCES AND ORGANISATION

You will need:-

- 1 table.

- A big box filled with interesting gift-wrapped presents of different shapes and sizes.

- A group of 8 or more preselected children to act out the story *The New Statue of Buddha.*

THE NEW STATUE OF BUDDHA
CAST
(Speaking parts)
Narrator
Monk 1
Monk 2
Monk 3
Monk 4, a young monk.
Merchant
Young Servant Girl
Old Monk

(Optional non speaking parts)
Monks
Men, women and children giving gifts to the monks.
Members of the household of the rich merchant.

PROPS
4 Begging bowls
Items of jewellery
Lots of gold coins
1 Small copper coin

COSTUMES are optional.

WHAT TO DO

Start the assembly by telling the children that we are going to be thinking about giving and sharing. Show them a big box and explain that it is full of presents of different shapes and sizes.

Ask the children if they can think of occasions when we give presents to each other.

They will probably suggest occasions such as birthdays, Christmas and other religious festivals like Davili and the Chinese new Year, to say thank-you and so on.

As a child gives a reason, ask him/her to choose a present from the box and to arrange it somewhere on the table next to the box.

When there is a good selection of gifts on the table ask the children to think about why we give presents on these occasions.

- QUESTION: Are all presents wrapped up nicely in a box or package?

- QUESTION: Are there some presents which cost nothing?

- QUESTION: What kind of gifts can we give which cost us nothing?

EXAMPLE: our time or effort.

- QUESTION: Do we always give to people we know?

- QUESTION: Can the children think of any charities which they, their parents or the school have given to?

Explain that many religions encourage people to give to others, especially to those people who are less fortunate or have less than us. Buddhism is one of these religions and began with the life of a great and wise teacher called **the Buddha**. The Buddha was born an Indian prince and spent his childhood living in a palace, surrounded by fine and beautiful possessions but in time he came to reject these. He talked about the importance of the gift of love and he encouraged people to show love and respect for all living things. The religion he founded spread to many countries of the world and is followed by many today.

Explain that there are many beautiful statues of The Buddha in temples throughout the world, and that you have chosen some children to act out a story about a statue which was made for a temple in China.

THE NEW STATUE OF BUDDHA

NARRATOR: A long time ago in China there was a Buddhist temple. The people living near the temple decided that it was time to made a new statue of the Buddha, for the one in the temple was very old now. So the monks of the temple decided to set out on a long journey around their great country, collecting gifts, so that they could make a bright new statue.

(Enter 4 MONKS with begging bowls.)

MONK 1: Brothers, let us travel the length and the breadth of our country asking for gifts so that we can build a beautiful new statue of our Buddha.

(MONKS walk off in different directions and start to collect gifts.)

NARRATOR: The monks travelled far and wide and collected many fine gifts. Most people gave gold or silver coins. Many women gave their favourite items of jewellery to be melted down. The monks were pleased that people were so generous and willing to share their belongings.

MONK 2: Look at all these gold coins.

MONK 3: Look at this fine necklace.

MONK 1: And this gold brooch.

(MONKS continue to collect coins and jewellery.)

NARRATOR: The youngest of the monks was very keen. He wanted to collect as much as he could to show how much he cared about the statue and to impress the other monks with his hard work. His final visit, before returning to the temple, was to the house of a very rich merchant.

MONK 4: I am sure this man will give generously.

(MEMBERS OF THE HOUSEHOLD gather.)

NARRATOR: The monk asked the whole household to assemble in the great hall, so that he could tell them all about the life of the Buddha. *(ENTER GIRL.)* He told them of the Buddha's wisdom and generosity. They listened intently, following his every word, even a young servant girl who worked in the kitchens came to hear him speak. Finally he asked them to give what they could afford towards the new statue. The rich merchant gave the monk a great many gold coins.

MERCHANT: *(Placing coins in begging bowl.)* Take these coins to help towards your statue.

(MERCHANT'S FRIENDS give coins and jewellery.)

NARRATOR: The merchant's friends gave more coins and the women gave fine jewellery - necklaces, bracelets earrings and brooches. The monk knew the others would be pleased with him when saw how much he had collected.

MONK 4: Thank you for your generous gifts. I must now return to the temple with all haste.

NARRATOR: As he was leaving the young servant girl ran up to him.

GIRL: *(Running up.)* Please take this copper coin. It is worth very little, I'm afraid, but it is all that I have and I would like to give it to the Buddha.

NARRATOR: The monk was in a hurry and he didn't really stop to think. He just wanted to get back to the temple and show the other monks how much he'd collected. He waved her away and hurried home.

(MONK 4 waves the GIRL away dismissively and turns to take a look at the begging bowl piled high with coins and overflowing with jewellery.)

MONK 4:   *(To himself.)* Just wait until they see how well I have done.

EXIT MONK 4 hurriedly. *To immediately* RE-ENTER WITH ALL THE OTHER MONKS.

NARRATOR: *(MONKS mime actions and reactions.)* The other monks were indeed pleased with the youngest monk. They collected all the gold and silver together and melted it down to make the statue of the Buddha. But, to their surprise and dismay, when the statue came out of the mould it was very ugly. They tried again but the same thing happened. Finally, one of the oldest monks stepped forward.

OLD MONK: *(Stepping forward.)* I think I know what has happened. This metal has been badly mixed and this is a sign that one of us has not shown enough love and kindness.

(MONKS look at one another. Pause.)

NARRATOR: The youngest monk stepped forward. *(Monk 4 steps forward and hangs his head in shame.)* He remembered how he had treated the young servant girl. He explained how he'd acted and went off to find the young girl and tell her that that they would be very grateful of her gift.

(Monk 4 finds the GIRL.)

NARRATOR: The young servant girl was delighted that she could give something towards the new statue.

MONK 4:   *(MONK 4 Accepts the copper coin from GIRL gratefully.)* Thank you for your gift.

(MONK 4 hurries back to the waiting MONKS.)

NARRATOR: *(As MONKS mime actions and reactions.)* The metal was melted down for the third time. This time the monks were not disappointed. *(GIRL, MERCHANT, HOUSEHOLD, and anyone who contributed all gather to view the statue.)* The statue was perfect and the people thought it looked magnificent. And in the middle of the Buddha's chest you could just see the little copper coin - the gift given with love from the young servant girl.

Kryssy Hurley
based on a traditional story

Ask the children watching what they think the story tells us about giving. Try to draw out that it is not always important what we give but the sentiment or reason behind the giving.

Finish the assembly with the following reflection.

REFLECTION

Help us to be generous and to share what we have with others. Help us to be more thoughtful of the needs of others and, in doing so, to realise the happiness we can find in giving.

ADDITIONAL RESOURCES AND ACTIVITIES

> The children could find out more about the life of Buddha and research the philosophy of Buddhism.

> The class could adopt a charity that they would like to raise money for.

> The children could design gift wrapping paper, perhaps using repeated patterns in a suitable computer program or repeat patterns using traditional methods like string printing or potato cuts.

> The children could write their own fables or parables.

> You could read the fable *The Ant and the Dove** Aesop - The Complete Fables, Penguin.

> > *Moral - giving and gratitude.

> You could read the parable of the Good Samaritan, St Luke, Chapter 10, verse 33, the New Testament, the Holy Bible.

> You could download *King Sivi,* a Birbal story about generosity. from the internet

> • Visit the website: **www.fundooz.com** .

> Many teachers explore feelings such as sharing and generosity through 'Circle Time' sessions in the classroom. Try this if you do not already undertake these activities.

> The children could find out about the many symbolic stories from different religions about the sharing of food.

> Discuss the effects of the National Lottery (Lotto) on fund-raising.

> Contact various charities like Christian Aid, Comic Relief, Oxfam and the NSPCC who have information packs to send out.

12. TRUTH AND TRUST

PSHE LINK: DEVELOPING GOOD RELATIONSHIPS

RESOURCES AND ORGANISATION

You will need:-

- A set of Call My Bluff Cards for the **Call My Bluff Game**.

- 4 Preselected children or children chosen on the day to read the definitions on the back of the Call My Bluff Cards.

- A set of 5 Trust Cards with the letters of TRUST written on the front and qualities on the reverse.

- 5 Children chosen on the day to read out the Trust Cards.

- A group of 6 + preselected children to act out a modern version of the *Cry Wolf* story.*

                                        *This is optional.

WHAT TO DO

Start the assembly by telling the children that they are going to play a game of **Call My Bluff**. Read out each word, holding up the card to show the word to the children watching, and each of the four chosen children can read out a definition for that word.

> Then ask the children watching to vote as to which definition is correct, before you reveal the correct answer.

Do this for each word.

NOTE: The Suggested Bluff Cards show the correct definition in bold or you can choose your own words and definitions if you prefer.

SUGGESTED BLUFF CARDS

CALL MY BLUFF

wurley

CALL MY BLUFF

1. **A native Australian hut**
2. A type of ice cream
3. A type of sea snail

CALL MY BLUFF

platitude

CALL MY BLUFF

1. Part of a satellite dish
2. A large plate used for serving vegetables
3. **Something which you say to help someone but it doesn't give them any real help**

CALL MY BLUFF

dwang

CALL MY BLUFF

1. **A large wrench for tightening nuts**
2. A stringed instrument
3. The name of a river

```
┌──────────────────────────────────────────┐
│ CALL MY BLUFF                              │
│                                            │
│                 southpaw                   │
│                                            │
│                                            │
│                            CALL MY BLUFF   │
└──────────────────────────────────────────┘
┌──────────────────────────────────────────┐
│                                            │
│    1.  A very small South American bear    │
│    2.  Someone who is left-handed          │
│    3.  A type of cactus                    │
│                                            │
└──────────────────────────────────────────┘
```

After this activity, explain to the children that in this game it is very difficult to know who is telling the truth. In life it can also be difficult, at times, to know who to trust or who is telling the truth.

Ask the children to suggest people in their lives who they feel they can trust.

EXAMPLE: your parents, your teacher, the police, etc.

Add that not all adults can be trusted, just because they are grown ups, and that trust needs to be earned. It does not just happen automatically.

Ask the children why it is important to tell the truth.

- QUESTION: What do they think the expression 'Honesty is the best policy' means and do they think it is true?

- QUESTION: How do they feel when they find out someone has lied to them?

Explain that telling the truth is an important part of many of the world's faiths.

EXAMPLE: The Ten Commandments given to Moses is important to both Jewish and Christian faiths. Exodus Chapter 20, the Old Testament, the Holy Bible.

Jesus speaks of the importance of truth and identifies himself with it. 'I am the way, the truth and the life:' St John, Chapter 14 verse 6, the New Testament, the Holy Bible.

Continue by reading a modern version of the *Cry Wolf* story.

NOTE ☐   You may wish to adapt this story so that it can be acted out by a group of children.

CRY WOLF!

It was the school holidays and Sally was bored. Her best friend, Sue, was on holiday in Florida, her mum was at work and she was left all on her own at home. She wanted something to do. She wanted something to happen. She wanted some excitement! She was fed up with watching television, listening to her CDs and painting pictures on her bedroom walls. She wanted a bit of action. In desperation, she phoned her mum.

'I'm bored, mum. What can I do?'

'Why don't you go for a bike ride? Or phone Mary and go swimming? You can take some money from the tin in the kitchen.'

'OK, mum.'

But Sally didn't want to go for a bike ride or go swimming with Mary. Anyway, Mary was boring. I think I'll have a bit of fun, she thought to herself! She picked up the phone, dialled and asked for the fire brigade.

'Help! Help! My house is on fire! You must come quickly and save me!'

Of course the fire engine arrived promptly and the firemen rushed into the house, looking for a fire. But of course there was none. Well, the Chief Fire Officer was not happy with Sally. He explained that calling the fire brigade out for nothing was a serious business because it might mean that they couldn't get to someone who was really in trouble. Sally said sorry and the firemen left. After they'd gone she started laughing.

'That was fun! What can I do now?'

This time she picked up the phone and asked for the police.

'Help! Please! There's a burglar in my house! Come quickly!'

Of course, the police car came very quickly and the police officers were not amused to find out that she'd only been joking. Again, she apologised and they left.

'I'm really having some fun now,' she said, 'What can I do next?'

This time she called for an ambulance.

'Help me! Help me! I think I've swallowed some poison! Come quickly!'

Well, you can guess what happened next. The ambulance came very quickly and the ambulance crew were surprised to see Sally sitting reading a magazine.

'Only joking!' she said.

The ambulance driver was not at all happy.

'You're the girl who called out the police, aren't you? And the fire brigade. We've heard all about you. What silly dangerous game do you think you're playing, young lady? This has got to stop now, or you're going to get yourself into serious trouble. Do you understand what I'm saying?'

'Yes, I understand. It's just that I was bored.'

'Well, you shouldn't be,' replied the ambulance driver. 'There are a hundred and one interesting things you could be doing. Now find yourself something to do that's not going to get you into trouble. Do you think you can do that?'

'Yes, I suppose so,' Sally replied. 'And, listen, I am really sorry. I hadn't realised I was causing so much trouble.'

The ambulance left. Sally felt a bit guilty. She hoped the police wouldn't tell her mum. Then she'd really be in trouble. Then she had an idea. She'd bake her mum a cake for when she came home.

So she set about baking a wonderful chocolate and vanilla cake. She thought her mum would be really pleased when she came home. She put the cake in the oven and went upstairs to watch television. What she didn't know was that she'd turned one of the cooker rings on as well, and there was a tea towel lying on top. Well, I expect you can guess what happened next.

Before long the whole kitchen was on fire. When Sally saw the smoke she phoned for the fire brigade and gave her name and number.

'Not you again,' said the Chief Fire Officer. 'Look, we're very busy and we certainly haven't got time for your silly games. Good-bye.'

'But I'm really in trouble!' she began, but he had already put the phone down.

By this time the flames were in the hallway and had started to creep up the stairs. Sally started to cry. She was sure she was going to die. At that moment she heard a voice at the bedroom window.

'Sally, are you in there?'

It was her neighbour. He had seen the smoke and had fetched a ladder to help her escape from the house.

'My wife has called the fire brigade. They'll be here any minute. They didn't seem very keen though, when I gave them the address. Very strange.'

As Sally climbed down the ladder her mum arrived home from work.

'What on earth has been happening here?' she cried.

'A bit too much excitement, mum. But it's all under control now.'

Kryssy Hurley

Ask the children what they think the message, or moral, is in that story.

Explain that the expression 'to cry wolf' comes from Aesop's fable The Shepherd's Boy and the Wolf.

THE SHEPHERD'S BOY AND THE WOLF

A Shepherd-Boy who watched a flock of sheep near a village brought out all the villagers three or four times by crying out, 'Wolf! Wolf!' and when the villagers came to help, he laughed at them. Then the Wolf really did come. The Shepherd-Boy, was really alarmed, and shouted in terror, 'Please, come and help me, the Wolf is killing the sheep', but no one paid any attention. So the Wolf was able to destroy the whole flock as the Shepherd-Boy looked on helplessly.

There is no believing a liar, even when he speaks the truth.

the Fables of Aesop

cry wolf raise repeated false alarms so a real one is disregarded.

Explain that telling the truth and being trustworthy are important whoever you are and whatever culture you belong to.

Discuss the idea of pretence.

EXAMPLE: fakes and forgeries.

Explain how it is better to be truthful even when the immediate consequences are not very pleasant.

EXAMPLE: cheating in exams, etc.

Finally, invite five children to hold up a Trust Card each with a letter of the word TRUST written on it. Ask each child in turn to read what is written on the back.

Explain that these are all things which are important when building up trust in a relationship.

TRUST CARDS

T

Try to keep secrets

R

Respect other people

U

Understand other people's points of view

S

Show that you are reliable and responsible

T

Tell the truth at all times

Finish the assembly with the following reflection.

REFLECTION

Help us to tell the truth and to be trustworthy. Also, help us to know who we can trust and rely on in our own lives.

ADDITIONAL RESOURCES AND ACTIVITIES

> The children could write their own stories, entitled, *Honesty is the Best Policy.*

> You could read the story about earning trust *B. B. Wolf* from *Parables for Little People* by Lawrence Castagnola, Resource Publications, Inc.

> The children could design and make their own burglar alarms.

> The children could find out about the local *Neighbourhood Watch*, if there is one.

SUMMER TERM

MY FRIENDS AND NEIGHBOURS

1. MY FRIENDS

PSHE LINK: DEVELOPING GOOD RELATIONSHIPS

RESOURCES AND ORGANISATION

You will need:-

- 7 large Friends Cards each one with a letter of the word FRIENDS written on it.

- A blank overhead transparency sheet and pens.*

  *This is optional.

- 4 Chairs at the front.*

  *1 Chair to be special if possible.

- Audience Cue Cards for the **Find-A-Friend** Game Show.

- Question and Answer Cards for the **Find-A-Friend** Game Show.

- 8 Children chosen beforehand or on the day - 7 to hold up the Friends Cards and 1 to rearrange the order of the cards.*
  * If the 7 children are preselected they can each write a quality that they consider important in a friend on one of the Friends Cards in class.

- 4 Contestants preselected and rehearsed or chosen on the day for the **Find-A-Friend** Game Show.*
  *Preselected children can think up and write their own questions.

WHAT TO DO

Have seven children standing at the front, each holding a Friends Card in random order.

> The order of the Friends Cards is jumbled ask for a volunteer to come up and rearrange the letters to form a word.

Explain that the assembly is about friendship and ask the children to suggest qualities that they think are important in a friend.

NOTE ☐ These qualities can be written up on an overhead transparency as you go along if you wish to refer back to them.

Listen to a range of suggestions.

NOTE ☐ Preselected children holding the cards up can each read out a quality that they look for in a friend.

EXAMPLE: 'I would like my friend to be able to make me laugh' or 'I would like my friend to enjoy playing the same games that I do', etc.

At this point, tell the children that they are going to have their own Game Show, called **Find-A-Friend**.

NOTE ☐ If the children have been preselected they can rehearse and possibly even invent their own Game Show questions beforehand. However, if less preparation is desired, children can be chosen on the day to read out cards written by the teacher or the suggested **Find-A-Friend** Question and Answer Cards.

> Explain to the children sitting down that they are the studio audience and agree on signals for them to clap, cheer, etc. Possibly holding up cue cards to make it more fun!

CUE CARDS

FIND-A-FRIEND
CLAP
CUE CARD

FIND-A-FRIEND
CHEER
CUE CARD

```
┌─────────────────────────────────────────┐
│ FIND-A-FRIEND                            │
│                                          │
│          CHANT FIND-A-FRIEND             │
│                                          │
│                            CUE CARD      │
└─────────────────────────────────────────┘
```

Explain that you are the Game Show host, and that you are going to choose four contestants from the studio audience. CONTESTANT 1 will sit on the special chair, to one side. This contestant is looking for a friend. CONTESTANT 2, CONTESTANT 3 and CONTESTANT 4 are possible friends and sit on the other three chairs. CONTESTANT 1 is going to ask each of the other contestants three questions in turn and listen carefully to their answers before deciding which one he/she will choose for a friend.

NOTE ☐ If this is not rehearsed cards can be given out to the three contestants with answers for them to read out. Here are some suggestions for questions and answers.

SUGGESTED QUESTION AND ANSWER CARDS

```
┌─────────────────────────────────────────┐
│  QUESTION 1 •                            │
│                                          │
│      If I was feeling really down what   │
│      would you do to cheer me up?        │
│                                          │
│                          FIND-A-FRIEND   │
├─────────────────────────────────────────┤
│  QUESTION 1 • ANSWER 1                   │
│                                          │
│  I'd go and play with someone else. I hate│
│  being around people who are miserable.  │
│                                          │
├─────────────────────────────────────────┤
│  QUESTION 1 • ANSWER 2                    │
│                                          │
│   I don't know. I suppose I'd leave you on│
│   your own until you were feeling better.│
│                                          │
└─────────────────────────────────────────┘
```

QUESTION 1 • **ANSWER 3**

I think I'd try to find out what was bothering you and if that didn't work I'd try to cheer you up by playing your favourite game.

QUESTION 2 •

If you won a big box of sweets in a competition what would you do?

FIND-A-FRIEND

QUESTION 2 • **ANSWER 1**

I wouldn't tell anyone.
I'd keep them all for myself.

QUESTION 2 • **ANSWER 2**

I would probably give my best friends one each then eat the rest myself.

QUESTION 2 • **ANSWER 3**

I would share them with my friends.

QUESTION 3 •

If I told you a really important secret could I trust you not to tell anyone?

FIND-A-FRIEND

QUESTION 3 • **ANSWER 1**

Well, I'd try not to tell anyone. But, surely,
it wouldn't matter if I just told a couple
of other people?

QUESTION 3 • **ANSWER 2**

I'd tell anyone who asked. Anyway they would
probably have found out eventually anyway.

QUESTION 3 • **ANSWER 3**

If I promised not to tell anyone I would
keep my word. I think trust is important.

When CONTESTANT 1 has chosen his/her friend you may wish
to go back to the list of qualities the children felt were
desirable in a friend and consider whether the chosen friend
satisfied any or all of them.

Explain to the children that finding good friends and having
good relationships are not quite as simple as just going on a
game show and picking them out.

EXAMPLE: Trust has to be earned.

Reflect on the qualities that they feel they like in their own
friends and how friendship is not just a one way relationship.

Finish the assembly with the following reflection.

REFLECTION

Let us give thanks for our friends and all the people who care
for us. Help us to be good friends, treating our friends as we
would wish to be treated. Let us spend a few moments
thinking about those qualities in our friends which make them
special to us.

ADDITIONAL RESOURCES AND ACTIVITIES

> A useful teacher resource is *Your World, My World* produced by Oxfam, Oxfam Education Resources for Schools. This is a photo pack which looks at the stories of four children from around the world and which considers the importance of family and friends.

> Another useful teacher resource to use with lower juniors is the story *The Sand Tray* by Don Rowe and Tim Archbold, Citizenship Foundation, A & C Black, London. This is a story which explores the concepts of friendship and fairness and which includes a list of suggested questions for discussion.

> The children could find out about greetings and friendship traditions from other cultures.

   EXAMPLE: giving leis (**lei** a Polynesian garland of flowers) to welcome visitors to Hawaii symbolises sharing.

> They could find out how to say 'Hello' in different languages. The *Euroquest* activity book has an activity page listing 'Hello' in the 11 official EU languages. For free copies of this publication or information about the European Union contact your local European Centre for Schools and Colleges.
   Publications Unit, European Commission, 8 Storey's Gate, London SW1P 3AT

> The children could design their own *'WANTED - A FRIEND!'* posters.

WANTED - A FRIEND

2. THINKING OF OTHERS

PSHE LINK: DEVELOPING GOOD RELATIONSHIPS
TAKING RESPONSIBILITY FOR THE NEEDS OF OTHERS
UNDERSTANDING THAT OUR ACTIONS AFFECT OURSELVES AND OTHERS
CARING ABOUT PEOPLE'S FEELINGS

RESOURCES AND ORGANISATION

You will need:-

• 1 tube of toothpaste and a plate.

• 1 chair and a woolly bobble hat.

• 9 Preselected children for the scene snippets.

• 1 Child rehearsed and chosen beforehand or chosen on the day to represent Mart's friend in the poem, 'Mart Was My Best Friend'.

• A group of rehearsed children to act out, 'Mart was My Best Friend'.*

*This is an optional alternative.

MART WAS MY BEST FRIEND
CAST
(Speaking parts)
Mart's Best friend
Mart
Mum

(Optional non-speaking parts)
Bus driver
Passengers
People waiting at the bus stop

WHAT TO DO

Explain to the children that they are going to watch several short scenes performed by groups of children.

NOTE ☐ These scene snippets can be as simple or as complex as you wish, depending on the time you choose to spend in preparation.

Ask the children to watch each scene carefully and to think about how some of the children involved could have acted differently in order to be better friends.

NOTE ☐ At the end of each scene the children acting can freeze and hold their positions, with the idea of moving swiftly from each scene snippet to the next.

EXAMPLE SCENE SNIPPETS

SCENE 1 A NEW CHILD AT SCHOOL • 3 CHILDREN
SCENE 2 GAME OF FOOTBALL   • 4 CHILDREN
SCENE 3 THE BIRTHDAY PRESENT   • 2 CHILDREN

1. A NEW CHILD AT SCHOOL

A new child to the school, approaches two children who are playing ball.

CHILD 1:   Hello. My name's Sam. I'm new here. Can I join in your game?

CHILD 2:   Go and ask someone else, we're busy.

CHILD 3:   Yeah, go away. This game's only meant for two people.

2. GAME OF FOOTBALL

Four children are about to organise a quick game of football in the school playground.

CHILD 1:   How about a quick game of footie?

CHILD 2:   Count me in.

CHILD 3:   I'll be on your team, John, because I was on Tim's last time.

CHILD 4:   OK, but we're not having your friend, Paul, on our team. He's hopeless at football. In fact, he's hopeless at everything really.

3. THE BIRTHDAY PRESENT

A girl hurries over to speak to her friend.

CHILD 1:   Hi, Sarah. Do you like my new skirt? It was a birthday present.

CHILD 2:   I had one of those last year. Nobody's wearing them any more. And anyway, it's a bit tight on you isn't it?

After the scene snippets have been performed, ask the actors if they felt they were acting as good friends. Ask the children who were watching if they thought any of the children could have acted in a different way.

- QUESTION: How might they feel if they were a new child, excluded from a game?

- QUESTION: How would they feel if they were criticised by their friend?

Encourage children to suggest some alternative actions or comments for each scene.

> Ask one child to come up to the front. Present him/her with the toothpaste tube and a plate.

Ask the child to squeeze out as much toothpaste as possible onto the plate. Then ask him/her to put the toothpaste back in the tube. This will, inevitably prove impossible and no doubt cause some amusement.

Explain to the children that sometimes we say things that we regret or wish we could take back but, like the toothpaste from the tube, it is not always easy to clean up the mess or to repair the damage.

> Ask the children to put up their hands if they have ever said something that they immediately wished they could take back.

Emphasise the importance of thinking about the consequence of our actions or comments before it is too late and damage is done to a friendship. Explain that, although friendship means thinking about the other person's feelings, there are bound to be times when we say or do something we wish we hadn't and that friendship is also about forgiving.

Tell the children that you are going to read them a poem by Michael Rosen, stopping at certain points to ask them what they think is going to happen.

Choose a child or ask the preselected child to sit in a chair at the front, wearing the woolly hat to represent Mart's friend.

NOTE ☐ If you have the preparation time, you may wish to select some children to act out the poem.

MART WAS MY BEST FRIEND

Mart was my best friend.
I thought he was great,
but one day he tried to do for me.

I had a hat - a woolly one
and I loved that hat.
It was warm and tight.
My mum had knitted it
and I wore it everywhere.

One day me and Mart were out
and we were standing at a bus stop
and suddenly
he goes and grabs my hat
and chucked it over the wall.
He thought I was going to go in there
and get it out.
He thought he'd make me do that
because he knew I liked that hat so much
I wouldn't be able to stand being without it.

- QUESTION: What do you think the boy in the poem is going
            to do now?

- QUESTION: What would you do in his position?

>   He was right -
>   I could hardly bear it.
>   I was really scared I'd never get it back.
>   But I never let on.
>   I never showed it on my face.
>   I just waited.
>
>   'Aren't you going to get your hat?'
>   he says.
>   'Your hat's gone,' he says.
>   'Your hat's over the wall.'
>   I looked the other way.
>
>   But I could still feel on my head
>   how he had pulled it off.
>   'Your hat's over the wall,' he says.
>   I didn't say a thing.
>
>   Then the bus came round the corner
>   at the end of the road.

- QUESTION: At this point, how do you think Mart is feeling?

- QUESTION: How would you feel if you were Mart and what
            would you do?

>   If I go home without my hat
>   I'm going to walk through the door
>   and mum's going to say
>   'Where's your hat?'
>   and if I say,
>   'It's over the wall,'
>   she's going to say,
>
>   'What's it doing there?'
>   and I'm going to say,
>   'Mart chucked it over,'
>   and she's going to say,
>   'Why didn't you go for it?'

'But you haven't left it there, have you?' she says.
'Yes,' I said.

'Well don't you ever come asking me to make you
something like that again.'
'You make me tired, you do.'

Later,
I was drinking some orange juice.
The front door-bell rang.

- QUESTION: Who do you think is at the door?

It was Mart.
He had the hat in his hand.
He handed it me - and went.

I shut the front door -
put on the hat
and walked into the kitchen.
Mum looked up.
'You don't need to wear your hat indoors do you?'
she said.
'I will for a bit,' I said.
And I did.

Michael Rosen

You Tell Me
Poems by Roger McGough and Michael Rosen 1979
Reproduced by permission of Penguin Books Ltd.

- QUESTION: Why do you think he wants to wear his hat in
            the house?

- QUESTION: Do you think Mart and the boy in the poem are
            good friends?

- QUESTION: What makes you think that Mart and the boy in
            the poem are good friends?

- QUESTION: Do you think the boy in the poem is still angry?
            with Mart at the end of the poem

Finish the assembly with the following reflection.

REFLECTION

Help us to be good friends and to care for the people around us. Sometimes we may upset someone by saying or doing something without really thinking and it is not always easy to put things right again. Let us remember that the things we say and do affect the people around us and that a smile or a friendly word cost nothing but can mean a lot to someone.

ADDITIONAL RESOURCES AND ACTIVITIES

> A very useful resource for exploring citizenship issues including friendships and relationships is *Introducing Citizenship* by Don Rowe, a book and video produced by A & C Black.

> The story *Joe's Car* by Annabelle Dixon & Tim Archbold, A & C Black looks at respecting other people's property.

> The children could write their own poems about times when they have argued or fallen out with one of their friends.

> In drama, the teacher could give groups of children Scene Starters with each scene starting with some kind of conflict. The children could then create and perform their own scene endings.

EXAMPLE: **SCENE STARTER 1.**

Daniel steals his friend Paul's new pencil case because he has always wanted one just like that. Their other friend Tom sees him do this ...

• QUESTION: How do the three boys deal with the situation?

SCENE STARTER 2.

Jenny has been invited to have tea with the new girl in the class, Katie, but she has already said that she will go shopping with her friend Susan. And, in any case, she doesn't think it'll be much fun at Katie's house anyway .....

• QUESTION: How does she deal with the situation?

> The children could paint or draw a friendly face. They could smile at one another and observe the results before they begin.

> Discuss with the children the way they make friends. e.g. suggesting interesting things to do together, by asking other people about themselves or sharing things.

> Further reading for children:
  Annie, The Invisible Girl, Rights of Children Series, Blackwell.
  Being Alone, Being Together, T. Berger, MacDonald.
  The Dancer, The Bear And The Nobody Boy, D. Bour, Black.
  Doctor Sean, P. Breinburg, Bodley Head.
  A Friend Can Help, T. Berger, MacDonald.
  Frisk The Unfriendly Foal, E. de Fossard, E.J. Arnold.
  Not Now Bernard, D. McKee, Anderson Press.
  The Rabbit's Wedding, G. Williams, Collins.
  How We Live, A. Harper, Kestrel.

3. SIGNS, SYMBOLS AND GESTURES

> PSHE LINK: DEVELOPING GOOD RELATIONSHIPS
> CARING ABOUT PEOPLE'S FEELINGS
> FEELING POSITIVE ABOUT THEMSELVES

RESOURCES AND ORGANISATION

You will need:-

- 1 Overhead transparency of a Smiley Face symbol - which a teacher might be use to praise effort or good work.

- A collection of signs, symbols and badges.

  NOTE ☐ These signs, symbols and badges can also be copied onto overhead transparencies if you wish.

- Something which has the school badge or coat of arms on.

- 6 Preselected children to present simple tableaux.

WHAT TO DO

> Start the assembly by putting up the overhead transparency of the Smiley Face, smiling as you do so, and be aware of the children's reactions.

Ask the children to describe what they see.

NOTE ☐ You will probably find that when the children see the Smiley Face, along with your own smile, most of them smile back at you.

Mention, briefly, the positive effect that a smile has on most people. Sometimes just the act of smiling oneself can make one feel better!

Ask the children how they feel when someone smiles at them.

NOTE □ If Smiley Faces are used in school, in children's exercise books, talk about what they signify. A Smiley Face sticker can be used to say that the teacher is very happy with a particular piece of work. Explain that the Smiley Face sticker is used as a symbol or sign of how he/she is feeling about a piece of work.

Explain that there are signs and symbols all around us in our everyday lives. In fact, it would be hard to go through life without using or responding to signs and symbols at all.

• QUESTION: Can the children give any examples of how signs or symbols have an important function in our lives?

Children may mention road signs or danger signs, warnings on medicines or danger signs near electricity installations.

> Show the children a selection of signs and symbols and ask if they can identify any of them.

EXAMPLES OF SIGNS AND SYMBOLS

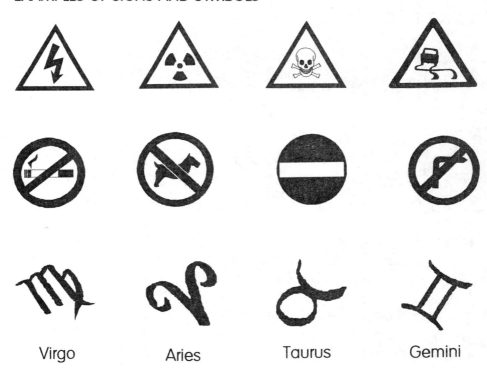

Virgo   Aries   Taurus   Gemini

Ask them if they think there is a difference between a sign and a symbol and what it might be.

If you wish, you can select some children to try to group the examples given into those which they think are signs and those which they think are symbols.

sign   a mark, symbol or device used to represent something or to distinguish the thing on which it is put. e.g. a jar marked with a sign.

symbol   1. a written or printed mark or character taken as the conventional sign that stands for or represents an object, abstract idea, function or process. e.g. the letters standing for the chemical elements, H Hydrogen, Mg Magnesium, Na Sodium, O Oxygen, etc. or the characters in musical notation. 2. emblem. e.g. the dove is a symbol of peace.

sign language   communication of thoughts or ideas by means of manual signs and gestures, used especially by the deaf.

Explain to the children that some people use sign language to communicate and that we use gestures and body language to communicate how we are feeling, often without realising. The way we move or make gestures can show our mood or how we are feeling about something or someone.

At this point explain to the children that you have some helpers who are each going to present a simple tableau which portrays a certain mood or feeling.

SUGGESTED TABLEAUX

BOREDOM • a child sitting, arms folded, slumped in a chair, gazing blankly ahead.

GREETING • a child waving.

EVERYTHING IS OK • a child showing a 'thumbs up'.

ANGER, RESENTMENT • a child frowning, arms folded.

DON'T KNOW, I GIVE UP • a child shrugging shoulders.

GREETING, WELCOME • a child smiling, arms open.

• QUESTION: Do they know how each of these children is feeling?

Explain that although none of the children in the tableaux have spoken we have at least some idea of the way they are feeling, just by looking at their body language or gesture.

Signs, symbols and gestures are all around us, both at home and at school. At school we have house colours or names, sports teams with their strips and our school badge or logo which may be found on uniforms, book bags and so on.

Explain that our school logo is part of our school identity and that we wear it or use it to show that we belong to our special school community.

NOTE ☐ If there is a school motto you may wish to mention this also.

> If practical, finish by getting the children to perform a Mexican wave around the assembly hall. See how controlled and quick you can make it, if necessary start by getting one section at a time to perform a mini-wave.

NOTE ☐ This does require concentration if done properly!

Finally, explain to the children that just as the Mexican wave spread rapidly around the hall a smile can be infectious too. Just as a stone creates ripples around it in a pond, a person wearing a smile or a friendly face will have a positive effect on those around.

Finish the assembly with the following reflection.

REFLECTION

Let us think about what gives our school its special identity. It is not just the buildings and equipment, but the **people** which make it a happy and stimulating place: the teachers, children and parents, and the many other people who help to take care of the school and make it what it is. Help us all to do our bit to keep our school special. And remember how easy it is to spread a smile!

ADDITIONAL RESOURCES AND ACTIVITIES

> In drama the children could explore mime. A useful resource is *Mime and Improvisation* by Alison Muir & Patricia Hammond, Oberon Books.

> The children could find out about sign language.

> The children could watch an except from a foreign language film and look at the way English subtitles are used or look at the way titles and exaggerated gestures are used in an old silent film.

> The children could explore signs within the context of religion, perhaps visiting a place of worship.

> The children could design their own class or school coat of arms.

> They could go on a sign hunt outside school or make up their own 'sign trails'.

173

4. CELEBRATING CULTURAL SIMILARITIES
AND DIFFERENCES

PSHE LINK: TO APPRECIATE THE RANGE OF IDENTITIES
WITHIN THE UK
AND TO CELEBRATE CULTURAL DIVERSITY
IN OUR WORLD

RESOURCES AND ORGANISATION

You will need:-

- Enough space in the collective worship area/hall to play 2 games.

- Statement Cards with children's statements or sample statements written on them. *
    * Statement Cards are optional as children can read their statements from sheets of paper if you prefer.

- 5 Preselected children to each read out a statement they have written about themselves.*
    * or the 5 preselected children or 5 chosen on the day to each read a sample statement.

- 6 or more players up to a maximum of 30 for each of the 2 games, **Gato Doente** and **Quin Es?**

WHAT TO DO

> Start the assembly by calling the preselected group of children to the front, to face the children watching.

They can then make a statement about themselves or read from a Statement Card one at a time. This statement can be about something which helps to make each one of them the individual that they are.

NOTE ☐ Or choose five children on the day to read out sample statements.

SAMPLE STATEMENT CARDS

STATEMENT CARDS

I can click my fingers

STATEMENT CARDS

I have brown hair and blue eyes

STATEMENT CARDS

I choose not to eat meat

STATEMENT CARDS

I'm a good swimmer

STATEMENT CARDS

I go to church on Sundays

Each of these children might like to share two or three facts about themselves. You may wish to link each child's facts.

EXAMPLE: I can't click my fingers but I can do a somersault.
I can do a somersault and walk on my bands, etc.

Explain to the children that every one of us is different and we all have special talents and abilities. Life would be very boring if we were all the same. Within our country, even within our school there are children who have different likes and dislikes, perhaps worship a different god or have different things which are special to them.

All over the world children are living very different lives, some of them in conditions much worse than those we are lucky enough to experience.

NOTE ☐ You may wish to make some topical reference here.

Some children are living in places where there is not enough food to eat or where they do not have a proper education. But in a lot of ways children are the same, with the same basic needs. All children love to play, whether they are lucky enough to have the latest computer game or whether they are playing a game they have made up which uses sticks and stones.

Explain that a group of children are going to help you to teach the children watching two games which are played in other parts of the world. Your helpers can demonstrate how to play the following games, as you explain the rules.

GATO DOENTE (SICK CAT)

This game comes from Brazil and can be played with as few as 6 players up to a maximum of 30. It can be played in a large hall or outdoors.

First of all one player is chosen to be the gato, or cat. The other players spread out. The gato chases the other children, as in a game of tag, and when he/she touches another player that player also becomes a gato doente or sick cat and must put their left hand over the part touched by the gato. This gato doente is then allowed to join the gato in chasing the other players, who also become gato doente if caught. The last player left is the winner.

QUIEN ES? (WHO IS IT?)

This game comes from Chile. It is also for 6 to 30 players and can be played in a large hall or outdoors.

The players stand in a line, one behind the other. The person at the head of the line is 'IT'. IT begins by asking the following questions:

IT: Han visto a mi amigo? Have you seen my friend?

OTHERS: No, Senor/Senora. No, Sir/Madam.

IT: Saben donda esta? Do you know where he/she is?

OTHERS: Si, Senor/Senora. Yes, Sir/Madam.

IT then slowly walks forward nine steps while all the OTHERS quickly change places behind him/her. One of them takes the place immediately behind IT.

OTHERS: (All call out) Quien es? Who is it?

IT must then ask three questions before guessing who it is.

EXAMPLE: • QUESTION 1. Is it a boy or a girl?
          • QUESTION 2. Is he dark or fair?
          • QUESTION 3. Is he tall?

The three players standing in line behind the 'friend' each give one word answers. Then IT must guess who is standing immediately behind. If he/she guesses correctly he/she has another turn at being IT. If not, the person standing immediately behind becomes IT.

Explain to the children that these are examples of games which can be played without any equipment and show that wherever children live and whatever equipment they have available to them they are able to invent and play their own games.

Suggest that the children might like to try out either of these games, try to find out about other games from different parts of the world or make up games of their own.

Finish the assembly with the following reflection.

REFLECTION

Let us think about the many similarities and differences which exist between the people of this earth and celebrate the things which make us special. Help us to understand and learn from each other.

ADDITIONAL RESOURCES AND ACTIVITIES

> Other games from around the world can be found in a booklet *Games For Summer Playtime* produced by UNICEF. Children could write off for this and then play the games. Oxfam, Live Aid and Sports Aid also have information packs.

> A very useful resource is *Aaagh to Zizz 135 Drama Games* by Graeme K. Talboys, Dramatic Lines. Many of these games can be used as part of a PSHE programme and all are easily adapted for formal and informal use.

> The children could be encouraged to make up their own playground games.

> The children could find out about The Declaration of the Rights of the Child adopted by the General Assembly of the United Nations.

1. Equality, regardless of race, religion, nationality or sex.
2. Special protection for full physical, intellectual, moral, spiritual and social development.
3. A name and nationality.
4. Adequate nutrition, housing and medical services.
5. Special care, if handicapped.
6. Love, understanding and protection.
7. Free education, play and recreation.
8. Be among the first to receive relief in times of disaster.
9. Protection against all forms of neglect, cruelty and exploitation.
10. Protection from any form of discrimination, and the right to be brought up in a spirit of universal brotherhood, peace and tolerance.

Do they think that all the children in the world are receiving this entitlement?

> A useful teacher resource which encourages respect for other cultures, and can be used with top infants and lower juniors, is the story *But Martin* by June Counsel, Faber and Faber.

> Read the fable *The Ant and the Chrysalis* * Aesop, *The Complete Fables*, Penguin.
> > * Moral - Appearances can be deceptive.

5. CHALLENGING STEREOTYPES AND JUDGING PEOPLE

PSHE LINK: TO ENCOURAGE RESPECT AND
UNDERSTANDING BETWEEN DIFFERENT RACES
TO CHALLENGE STEREOTYPES

RESOURCES AND ORGANISATION

You will need:-

- A box containing: a young child's story book, a bottle of wine, a box of chocolates, a toy, a bottle of medicine.

- 5 Large pictures or photographs of people of different ages and gender.

- 5 Large card Profession Labels.

PROFESSION LABELS

PROFESSION LABELS

doctor

PROFESSION LABELS

nurse

PROFESSION LABELS

pilot

```
┌──────────────────────────────────┐
│ PROFESSION LABELS                  │
│                                    │
│            student                 │
│                                    │
│                                    │
└──────────────────────────────────┘
```

```
┌──────────────────────────────────┐
│ PROFESSION LABELS                  │
│                                    │
│           bus driver               │
│                                    │
│                                    │
└──────────────────────────────────┘
```

- 8 Ribbons 2 red, blue, yellow and green.*

  *Team bands will do.

- 3 Small tables or chairs to display water, food and wood.

- Bottles of water, a selection of fruit and vegetables, a pile of twigs or wood.

- 1 Small tent or some form of shelter.

- 1 Overhead transparency picture of a man reaching to pull a woman away from a bus and to safety.

- 10 Children chosen on the day - 1 group of 5 to hold up objects and pictures and the second group to hold up Profession Labels.

- 9 Preselected children to act out or dance the 'Rainbow Folk' poem.*

  * or children chosen on the day to share things out and combine ribbons.

WHAT TO DO

> Start the assembly by choosing five children to hold up the story book, the bottle of wine, box of chocolates, the toy and the bottle of medicine.

Ask the other children if they can identify what each of the children is holding and describe what it might be like inside.

When they have identified each item ask them how they were able to tell so easily what each item was.

NOTE ☐ They may suggest pictures, writing, signs or symbols as clues.

Explain that it was easy to say what was inside each item because there were many obvious visual clues.

EXAMPLE VISUAL CLUES

- The cover of the book had pictures which would appeal to a young child.

- The medicine bottle had a chemist's label with dosage instructions.

- The label on the wine bottle had the type of wine, name of the wine producer, country of origin and year of production on the label.

Next take back the items and give each child a picture of a person instead.

Choose 5 more children and give each one a label with a profession written on it. Ask these children to try to match one Profession Label with each picture.

NOTE ☐ They may find this quite difficult, but insist that they find a match for each label.

Tell the children with the labels to stand next to their chosen picture.

> Ask the other children to put their hands up if they agree or disagree with the choices made.

Ask some of the children at the front to justify their choices.

Explain to the children that it was not a very fair exercise as there is no way of knowing which label goes with which person. Sometimes in life we make judgements about people because of the way they look, their age or sex but we must be very careful that we don't just judge people by the way they look alone.

Rearrange the labels a couple of times to show that, in fact, any of the labels could have gone with any of the pictures. Allow the children helping to return to their places.

Sum up by saying that whilst appearances are important and undoubtedly do make an impression on us judging someone by the way they look can be misleading and sometimes dangerous. Explain to the children what the word 'stereotype' means and ask them to describe some stereotypes.

stereotype   1. to conform to a type. 2. a person, group or thing that conforms to an unjustifiably fixed, standardised, mental picture. 3. a fixed or conventional notion or conception of a person, group or thing.

EXAMPLE: A teenager, football supporters, bikers, a shark, etc.

Explain to the children that you are going to read them a poem about some people who made the mistake of judging each other by their appearance.

Put the food, water, twigs and shelter in four different areas, using the tables or chairs so that they can be seen.

> Invite the preselected children to step forward.

NOTE ☐ Or choose nine children to come to the front.

> Give out ribbons to eight of the children and let the ninth stand to one side for the moment.

BLUE   • The 2 children with the blue ribbons can stand by the table with the food.

GREEN • The 2 greens can stand by the table with the food.

RED   • The 2 reds can stand by the water.

YELLOW • The 2 yellows can stand by the shelter.

NOTE ☐   If you choose the children beforehand you may like to dramatise the poem or put your own dance/movement sequence to the words. If you choose children on the day of the assembly, you may just get them to combine their ribbons at the end after they have shared out their food, water, etc.

RAINBOW FOLK

The world was created and all remained still,
Mountain and lake, dark forest and hill.
Animals, plants, created with love,
Rivers and seas, skies up above.
The creator made people to care for his place,
Men, women, children with plenty of space.
And one day a warm wind blew over the land,
Across the green forests and deserts of sand.
It filled them with love and a yearning to live,
To care for each other, to respect and to give.
And so they all lived for many a year,
Exploring their world with nothing to fear.
Until one day, with surprise they all found,
Colourful ribbons scattered over the ground.
They were filled with excitement, the ribbons so bright,
They played with them merrily, from daybreak to night.
Then one had an idea, when sitting alone,
They should each choose a colour and make it their own.
So some chose red, to thread through their hair,
Or yellow or green round their waists they would wear.
And some preferred blue, like the sky up above,
So they all had a ribbon, chosen with love.
Suddenly another wind, blustery and bold,
Blew through the land, made them shiver with cold.
They looked at each other, gazed hard and long,
They noticed their differences, something was wrong.
No laughter, no playing between brother and brother,
No caring, no sharing, no trusting each other.
They gathered in groups, each colour apart,
And ran to four corners, heavy of heart.
They forgot they'd been friends and the life that they'd shared,
Each colour lived separately, and nobody cared.
They built walls around them, to keep out the others,
And all those alike were now treated as brothers.
So they lived for a while in their separate lands,
In the forests of dark or the deserts of sands.
The blues in a valley, with plenty to eat,
The greens near the forest, round a fire they would eat.
The yellows in a cave, sheltered from the weather,
And the reds made their homes by the river together.
But as time went on and they'd done what they could,
The reds needed shelter and the yellows needed wood.
And the blues found that water was in short supply,
And the greens needed food or else they would die.

But they were all too afraid to seek help from the rest,
When a stranger appeared and said, 'I know what's best.'
'Share what you have, that way you'll survive.
Pool your resources to help keep you alive.
Try working together, yellow with red,
Not avoiding each other but helping instead.'
Then one of the greens said, 'These ribbons must go.
They started our problems, that we all know.'
'But we'll all miss their brightness, it's certainly clear,'
Said a blue, 'I'm beginning to have an idea.'
'Why don't we weave them into one rainbow strand,
To celebrate our differences and unite our fine land.'
'That,' said the stranger, 'is what's best I am sure.
It will bind you together and bring peace once more.'
And so they all lived with acceptance and joy,
Celebrating their differences, each girl and boy.
As they worked together their happiness would increase,
Their bright rainbow ribbon a symbol of peace.

Kryssy Hurley

Explain that you are now going to show the children half an overhead transparency picture and you would like them to try to guess what is about to happen.

NOTE ☐ When only half the picture is seen it appears that the man is reaching out to grab the woman's handbag or her purse. However, when the whole picture is seen it becomes obvious that the man is not trying to steal her purse, but reaching out to pull her away from an oncoming bus.

The children may be surprised when they see the whole picture and realise that only seeing part of the picture misled them. Stress that it is easy to make judgements sometimes when we do not have the whole picture just as it can be all too easy to judge people on appearances alone.

Finish the assembly with the following reflection.

REFLECTION

Help us to judge people fairly and not to make hasty judgements because of their appearance or because of something we may have heard about them. The world would be a very dull place if we were all the same. Let us celebrate those things which make us different and which make each one of us special.

ADDITIONAL RESOURCES AND ACTIVITIES

> A useful teacher resource to use with juniors is the story 'The Man Whose Mother Was a Pirate' Margaret Mahy, Puffin, which encourages exploration of issues such as stereotyping.

> The children could make their own whole/half pictures, with a flap to reveal the rest of the picture and situation.

  EXAMPLE: A child appears to be viciously kicking somebody. However, when the whole picture is revealed the child is seen to be playing football.

  A child is standing close to a broken window looking shocked and appears to be the culprit. However, when the whole picture is revealed the culprit is seen running away.

> The children could write their own stories about people who have been treated unfairly because of stereotyping.

> Further reading for children: No Two Zebras Are The Same, J. Anderson, Lion Publishing. Frances Face Maker, W. Cole, Magnet. The Boy With Two Eyes, Rights of Children Series, Blackwell. The Elephant With Rosy-Coloured Ears, B. Resch, Black. Straight Hair, Curly Hair, A. Goldin, Black. Your Skin And Mine, P. Showers, Black.

6. LET'S COMMUNICATE

PSHE LINK: TALKING AND WRITING ABOUT THEIR OPINIONS
EXPLAINING THEIR VIEWS

RESOURCES AND ORGANISATION

You will need:-

- 13 Communication Cards each with a letter of the word COMMUNICATION on the front.

- Sample styles of communication written on the backs of the Communication Cards.*

    *or the children's own examples.

- 1 Flip chart or overhead projector with a blank transparency and marker pen.

- 13 Children chosen on the day to hold up the Communication Cards and to assist you.*
    *or preselected children who have written their own examples of styles of communication in class.

- A group of 6 + rehearsed children to act out 'Chinese Whispers'. *

    * This is optional.

CHINESE WHISPERS
CAST
(Speaking parts)
Jenny
Jim
Rachel
Claire
Alice
John

No set, props or costumes are required.

WHAT TO DO

Start the assembly by telling the children that they are going to be thinking about communication in today's assembly.

> Choose thirteen children to come to the front, giving each one a communication card with a letter on it and then ask them to rearrange themselves to make the word **COMMUNICATION**.

Ask the children watching how your helpers managed to rearrange themselves so quickly.

NOTE ☐ They will probably suggest 'talking to each other' or 'showing each other where to stand by pointing'.

Go on to explain that the children with the letters could never have rearranged themselves without communicating with each other in some way, that we are all communicating with each other every day and that there are many different ways in which we can do this.

NOTE ☐ If this is an assembly which you have prepared with your class, you may wish to involve more children in the following activities, drawing on some of their own ideas from work in class or in drama sessions.

If, however, this is a teacher led assembly and you have limited preparation time you can use the following ideas as an outline for your assembly.

Ask the children to suggest ways in which we communicate.

EXAMPLE: talking, writing letters and e-mails, sending faxes or text messages, Morse code, sign language, etc.

NOTE ☐ Record these on the flip chart or overhead transparency.

You might also like to show the children some examples of the different ways in which we communicate.

EXAMPLE: SIGN LANGUAGE

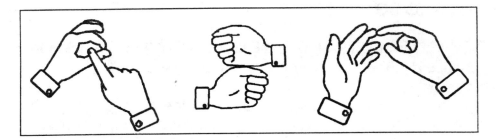

Explain that one of the most important and effective ways of communicating is by speech. In fact, we often don't realise how much we rely on speech until we lose our voice, take part in a sponsored silence or visit a foreign country where we don't understand the language. Speech is a powerful tool which can be used in many ways.

> At this point bring back the Communication Card holders and ask them all to look on the back of the cards and read out the words.

SAMPLE COMMUNICATION CARDS

COMMUNICATION CARDS
C

complain

COMMUNICATION CARDS
O

ask

COMMUNICATION CARDS

M

tell off

COMMUNICATION CARDS

M

explain

COMMUNICATION CARDS

U

give an opinion

COMMUNICATION CARDS

N

compliment

COMMUNICATION CARDS
I

answer

COMMUNICATION CARDS
C

criticise

COMMUNICATION CARDS
A

insult

COMMUNICATION CARDS
T

praise

```
COMMUNICATION CARDS

          I
```

```
          question
```

```
COMMUNICATION CARDS

          O
```

```
       give an account
```

```
COMMUNICATION CARDS

          N
```

```
       give instructions
```

> Act out or read out the various styles of communication one
  at a time and encourage the children to identify which card
  each relates to.

As each example is given the child with the appropriate card
can sit down.

NOTE ☐ If you wish to involve more children they can prepare
      additional examples of their own before the day of
      the assembly to go with these thirteen
      Communication Cards.

Continue by reading a story which demonstrates how speech can sometimes mislead.

NOTE □ Alternatively the story 'Chinese Whispers' can be dramatised and acted out by a group of children.

CHINESE WHISPERS

One day, at morning playtime, Jenny was admiring Jim's new baseball cap.
'Hey, it's really cool,' she said, 'I wish I had one like that.'

Now Jim rather liked Jenny and as he was keen to impress her he said that she could wear his cap for the rest of the day and give it back to him at the end of school.

Jenny was really pleased and ran to tell her friend, Rachel.
'Hey, Rachel, guess what? Jim has lent me his cap for the afternoon.'
'That's nice of him,' said Rachel.

Later that morning, Rachel told one of her friends what Jim had done.
'Hey, Claire, Jim's given Jenny his baseball cap.'
'Wow!' said Claire, 'That's nice.'

When Claire saw her friend, Alice, she told her the news.
'Jim's bought Claire a new hat, you know!'
Alice was impressed.

Later that day, Alice was chatting to John.
'You know, John, Jenny's really lucky to have Jim for a friend.'
'Why's that?' John asked. 'He buys her clothes and really nice presents.'
'Really!' exclaimed John, 'I didn't know.'

At the end of the school day, Jenny returned the cap to Jim and walked home with Rachel. Jim walked home with his friend, John.
'Let's stop at the shop and buy some sweets,' suggested John.
'Sorry, I can't today. I haven't got any money,' Jim said.

'Well, I'm not surprised,' said John, 'after all those presents you've bought for Jenny.'

Kryssy Hurley

Discuss the story with the children, pointing out that, like the game Chinese Whispers, stories can sometimes be changed or distorted as they are told. Although the power of speech can be positive and helpful there are times when it can be misleading or even hurtful. Speech is a useful and powerful means of communication but it is up to us how we use it!

Continue by reading the following humorous poem:

TALK'S CHEAP

They say, talk's cheap,
But whoever heard of a shop selling half a kilogram of chatter
or a bumper box of conversation?
They say that money talks,
But I've yet to hear a five pound note answer me back.
They say, 'Speak out, speak up boy!'
But I'd love to surprise them by speaking in
or speaking down to them.
'Oh, he's all talk,' they moan.
And I imagine a man made up entirely of words,
from his head to his question mark toes.
My mum says, '**Think** before you speak,'
But I'm sure it's not possible to speak without thinking.
They tell me to speak my mind,
But my mind's so busy and full of questions
that I'm afraid it would take all day.
They say, 'Now you're talking, mate!'
Well, what was I doing before, then?
And when they say, 'Strictly speaking,'
I think they must be talking about my teacher,
'cos she's quite strict.
They say, 'Small talk,'
But I've never heard of big talk.
And I think I've missed out 'cos
I've never actually seen anyone talking out of their hat.
And apparently Mrs Jones' new sports car is the talk of the town,

But everyone knows towns, unlike money, can't talk.
What do you think?
Personally, I think it's all talk,
And, as we all know, talk's cheap!

Kryssy Hurley

Finish the assembly with the following reflection.

REFLECTION

Let us think about the different ways in which we are able to communicate. Help us to appreciate our power of speech and to use it to do good and to make the most of abilities. Help us to learn and to explore our world, to express our opinions thoughtfully, to encourage rather than criticise and to be kind rather than be hurtful.

ADDITIONAL RESOURCES AND ACTIVITIES

> A visitor could be invited into school to talk to the children about sign language.

> The children could look at the type of language used in text messaging and make comparisons with more formal writing and spelling conventions.

> The children could communicate with each other using Morse code.

> The children could write pen-friend letters.

   NOTE ☐ You might like to develop the idea by making a 'letterbox'. Then letters could be 'posted' to 'pen-friends' within the school.

> Take in local newspapers for the children to find out about local issues. Then you could mock-up a Readers Letters page for children to 'write in' with their own observations, comments and protests about local issues.

> The children could put together a wall display on the theme of communication.

> Read the fable *The North Wind and the Sun* * Aesop The Complete Fables, Penguin.
> * Moral - Gentle persuasion is sometimes better than violence.

> Discuss when it's helpful to speak quietly and when it's helpful to speak loudly and how loudness and softness adds to the meaning of any communication.

> Discuss the need to listen to others as well as wanting people to listen to us.

> Discuss the problem of communication when there is a difference of language. Then the children can explore the ways of communicating if they do not understand someone's language. e.g. pointing, miming, making approving noises when someone repeats the correct name of an object or person.

> The children could act out showing a visitor round parts of the school.

> Discuss ways of communicating other than talking. e.g. fax messages, e-mail, semaphore, smoke signals, flags, lights, newspapers, books, theatre, film, music, art.

> The children could find out how different religious leaders communicated their beliefs.

7. DON'T BE A BULLY!

> PSHE LINK: TO REALISE THE CONSEQUENCES OF
> ANTI-SOCIAL AND AGGRESSIVE BEHAVIOUR
> SUCH AS BULLYING AND RACISM

RESOURCES AND ORGANISATION

You will need:-

- 1 Picture or object which symbolises peace.

- Pictures and additional information on the life of Martin Luther King.*

                                                              * This is optional.

- Preselected children to read pieces they have previously written in class on the subject of 'Utopia'.

WHAT TO DO

Start the assembly by reminding the children about some recent assemblies, where we thought about similarities and differences between different cultures and reflected on how important it is not to judge people because they may seem different to us. Explain that in today's assembly we are going to think about the consequences of behaviour such as bullying and racism and learn something about people who have felt strongly about this world issue.

Next tell the children the story of Martin Luther King.

NOTE   ☐   You may wish to use a reference book and go into much greater detail.

MARTIN LUTHER KING

Martin Luther King was born in 1929 in the United States of America. He grew up in the southern state of Georgia, where, at that time, black people did not have the same rights as white people. It was very common to see signs which read, 'WHITES ONLY' or 'NO COLOURED'. This shocked and upset Martin Luther King, as he believed all people should be treated equally, regardless of their skin colour.

Even on the buses, there were separate seats for whites and blacks. On one occasion, a black lady called Rosa Parks refused to give up her seat for a white person and for this reason alone was arrested and put into prison. Dr King joined a protest meeting where the black people of the town decided that they would not use the buses until they were allowed to choose where they would sit.

Eventually they achieved this but their fight for equal rights continued. Black people believed they had a right to mix with white people in all other public places. Dr King spoke many times about his beliefs and encouraged people to fight for equal rights using peaceful means. He was often attacked, criticised and even thrown into jail but this did not put him off. In one of his speeches for peace Martin Luther King once said:

'I have a dream, that one day this nation will rise up and live out it's belief that all men are created equal. I have a dream that my four little children will one day live in a nation where they will not be judged by the colour of their skin but by their character.'

In 1964 Martin Luther King was awarded the Nobel Peace prize and his campaign contributed to the passing of the Civil Rights Act in 1964 and the Voting Rights Act in 1965.

Martin Luther King made many good friends in his lifetime but sadly he made enemies too, one of whom shot him as he stood on his hotel balcony in Memphis, Tennessee.

Martin Luther King Jr. 1929-68, born in Atlanta, the son of a Baptist minister he became pastor of Dexter Avenue Baptist Church, Montgomery, Alabama preaching non-violence and campaigning constantly to end segregation in the South. The clergyman and leader of the Negro civil rights movement was assassinated by James Earl Ray. In his honour the 3rd Monday in January is a public holiday in the U.S.A.

Just as Martin Luther King had a dream or a vision of how he would like his country to be, many people throughout history have had ideas of what a perfect world would be like. These perfect worlds are often called Utopia, a word derived from the Greek ou not + topos place meaning 'good place' or 'no place'.

Utopia   1. an imagined perfect place or state of things. 2. any visionary scheme or system for an ideally perfect society. The word was first used as the name of an imagined island having a perfect political and social system in the book *Utopia* by Sir Thomas More, written in 1516.

Explain to the children watching that a group of children would like to share their ideas and visions of a perfect world or Utopia.

NOTE ☐ These pieces are likely to emerge from work done in class in RE or PSHE.

As the group of children read out their ideas and thoughts on Utopia, each individual can hold the symbol of peace which is passed on to each new child who speaks.

EXAMPLE: An olive branch or an image of a dove, etc.

NOTE ☐ You will need to explain to the children watching the significance of the symbol.

Finish the assembly with the following reflection.

REFLECTION

Ask the children to reflect on the meaning of the following extract from the American poet Henry Wadsworth Longfellow's poem, 'The Song of Hiawatha', written in 1855 - mentioning that, sadly, anger and war between different peoples is not merely a problem of recent history.

THE SONG OF HIAWATHA

'I have given you lands to hunt in,
I have given you streams to fish in,

I have given you bear and bison,
I have given you roe and reindeer,
I have given you brant* and beaver,
Filled the marshes full of wild-fowl,
Filled the rivers full of fishes,
Why then are you not contented?
Why then will you hunt each other?
I am weary of your quarrels,
Weary of your wars and bloodshed,
Weary of your prayers for vengeance,
Of your wranglings and dissensions;
All your strength is in your union,
All your danger is in discord;
Hencefore be at peace henceforward.
And as brothers live together.'

Henry Wadsworth Longfellow

*small, dark wild geese of North America and Canada.

ADDITIONAL RESOURCES AND ACTIVITIES

> This assembly could form part of PSHE work in class and links could be made with the school behaviour and anti-racist policies on issues such as Bullying and Racism. The children could discuss strategies which may be useful for dealing with bullying within school.

> The children could research the life of Martin Luther King.

> The children could write poems or prose about Utopia.

> The children could all work together to create their own Utopia painting, montage frieze or model.

> The following books are all useful teacher resources:
  BULLYING THEME:
   • *Willy the Champ, Willy the Wimp*, Anthony Browne, Walker Books.
   • *The Bad Tempered Ladybird*, Eric Carle, Hamish Hamilton Ltd.
  PREJUDICE AND INTOLERANCE THEME:
   • *Tusk, Tusk*, David McKee, Red Fox.
  GANGING UP AND NAME CALLING THEME:
   • *Hurrah for Ethelyn*, Babette, Mammoth.

8. WHAT A TEAM!

PSHE LINK: TO FEEL POSITIVE ABOUT THEMSELVES

RESOURCES AND ORGANISATION

You will need:-

- 1 blank overhead transparency sheet or several medium sized pieces of card and a marker pen*

    *and/or use the pre-written Qualities Cards.

- 4 Pre-written Qualities Cards.

- A rope and an old telephone directory.

- 7 Preselected children to take part in the tug of war - 4 for the Do-Your-Own-Thing Team and 3 for the Working-Together Team

- A group of preselected children with relevant badges, logos and mascots who can talk about the club or team they belong to.

- 2 Children to take part in the Telephone Directory Challenge.

WHAT TO DO

Start the assembly by introducing the two tug of war teams.

TUG OF WAR

HOST: On my right we have the three members of the **Working-Together Team**. And they've come all the way from Asoneton. On my left, from Separatesville, we have the slightly larger team of **Do-Your-Own-Thing**. Four against three, a slightly unfair contest you may say, but the **Working-Together Team** come here today with a lot of wins behind them, so anything could happen!

Ask the children watching to predict which team they think will win and to say why.

HOST: Stand back, please, and let our teams take the strain of the rope! Three, . . . two, ... And off you go!

At first the team from Separatesville can take the lead, on account of their greater number. Then things start to change! One member of the Separatesville team announces that he/she is tired and has decided to give up and walks away. Another member announces that he/she has to go as he/she has got something else to do and also walks away. The team from Asoneton starts to take a slight lead. Finally two members of the Separatesville team start to argue about whether it would be a good idea to swap sides as the other team looks more like winning! After a few more tense moments the team from Asoneton wins.

Discuss with the children why they think the team from Asoneton finally won, in spite of being fewer in number. Point out that the team members from Asoneton worked together to win the tug of war, whilst the other team, like their name, acted as individuals, doing their own thing.

Get the **Working-Together Team** to stand up again. Ask the children watching what it means to be a team member and what qualities they think are important for a team member.

NOTE   ☐ Write these qualities on the blank overhead transparency or pieces of card for the **Working-Together Team** to hold up or use the sample Qualities Cards if you wish.

SAMPLE QUALITIES CARDS

QUALITIES CARDS

co-operation

```
┌─────────────────────────────────────────┐
│ QUALITIES CARDS                           │
│                                           │
│    working towards the same goal          │
│                                           │
│                                           │
└─────────────────────────────────────────┘
```

```
┌─────────────────────────────────────────┐
│ QUALITIES CARDS                           │
│                                           │
│              perseverance                 │
│                                           │
│                                           │
└─────────────────────────────────────────┘
```

```
┌─────────────────────────────────────────┐
│ QUALITIES CARDS                           │
│                                           │
│                loyalty                    │
│                                           │
└─────────────────────────────────────────┘
```

> At this point invite a small group of children up to the front, to talk about teams that they belong to.

EXAMPLE: Football team, rugby team, cricket team, hockey team, etc.

Encourage them to show their badges/logos/mascots and if possible explain how members of their team work together. i.e. If it is a sport, they may have a special role within that team.

NOTE ☐ You may wish to invite members of one of the school teams to explain the positions they play in and to give examples of winning as a direct result of working together.

EXAMPLE: Each player in a basketball or netball team has a slightly different role and each is equally important. The goal shooter could not score if the rest of the team were not working together to get the ball to him/her.

Finally invite a couple of children up to the front to undertake The Telephone Directory Challenge.

THE TELEPHONE DIRECTORY CHALLENGE

The challenge is to tear the directory in half, in one go. Take one page yourself and tear it in half, to show how thin the paper is. The children will not be able to tear the whole book in half in one go and will probably realise this straight away.

Ask them to explain what makes the book so hard to tear.

NOTE ☐ They will probably tell you that one page on its own is much easier to tear than lots of pages together.

Conclude by saying that the toughness of the book comes from its combined pages just as the strength of a good team comes from the members working as one, not as individuals.

Finish the assembly with the following reflection.

REFLECTION

The strength of a great rope comes from the many smaller strands it is made up of.
The strength of a mighty forest comes from the individual trees which grow in it.
The strength and success of a good football team come from individual players working as one.

We all have a place in our school community and we all have a part to play, depending on our different talents and skills. Help us also to work together, in co-operation, as a good team does.

ADDITIONAL RESOURCES AND ACTIVITIES

> The children could play some different team games in games lessons, perhaps inventing some of their own. A useful source of interesting and unusual team games is *Aaargh to Zizz 135 Drama Games*, Graeme K. Talboys, Dramatic Lines.

> The children could bring in pictures and information on their favourite teams.

> The children could put together a 'Dream Team' of football players they think would work well together.

> Teams of children could carry out problem solving activities which rely on co-operation. e.g. using crates, ropes, etc. to get across an imaginary swamp.

> The children could find out how creatures co-operate in different ways. e.g. two shire horses, an older one and a younger one, working in harness, oxen pulling together to lighten the load, etc. Then they could look at the part humans play in these examples. Bees and ants also provide interesting patterns of working together.

> The children could list qualities and skills that are needed to make good group members for particular activities. e.g. if they had to design and make a wooden playhouse for the school playground, who would they pick and why?

> Press cuttings of any recent disaster can provide useful examples of people working as teams to help others. Charities such as Oxfam, Save The Children Fund and Christian Aid will often send speakers into school to talk about their work.

> Jesus had a team of people, his disciples, to help spread the Gospel. The children could find out about religious leaders and their followers and how they co-operated and supported one another. They could also look at other types of leaders and their followers. e.g. political leaders, kings and queens, etc.

9. TALENT AND ABILITY

> PSHE LINK: TO DEVELOP CONFIDENCE. AND RESPONSIBILITY
> TO MAKE THE MOST OF OUR ABILITIES AND
> TO RECOGNISE OUR WORTH AS INDIVIDUALS

RESOURCES AND ORGANISATION

You will need:-

- Pictures to put up during the *The Self-Important Lion* story. *
  * This is optional.

- A group of children to demonstrate some of their talents/abilities.

WHAT TO DO

Start the assembly by explaining to the children that they are going to be thinking about talents and abilities and how we can make the most of ours. Explain that everyone has different abilities and talents and the important thing is, that we are making the most of our own abilities.

Tell the children that you are going to start by telling them a story about a lion who thought he was very important and talented but found out that he wasn't the only one to have special and useful talents.

THE SELF-IMPORTANT LION

There once was a lion called Rex and he lived deep in the lush and tangled green jungle, somewhere hot and tropical. Rex had given himself the name 'Rex' because it meant 'king' and he'd heard ancient stories say that the lion is, without doubt, king of the jungle.

Now Rex felt that he really was the most important creature living in the jungle and he was forever reminding the other animals of this. He would play loud lion-like music, raise his giant paws towards the sky and chant the following rap-like ditty.

REX'S RAP

My name is Rex,
And it don't need no test,
To show you other animals,
That I am the best.
I'm strong, I'm smart,
And, hey dude, I'm cool,
I'm the king of the jungle,
I ain't no fool.

And the more Rex chanted his little rhyme, the more he believed it. As for the other animals, well, Rex was big and strong and, as the ancient tales said, the lion **was** the king of the jungle and to be respected at all times. So when Rex's bragging annoyed the other animals or when he teased them for being weak and useless they dared not argue. As time went on Rex became more and more conceited and full of himself.

One day a stranger arrived in that part of the jungle, telling of great treasure, guarded by a fierce and wicked troll. The animals listened in awe, as the stranger told of fine rubies, sparkling diamonds and more gold than they would ever live to see. Rex was listening very carefully and as soon as the stranger had finished talking he announced to the other animals that he intended to steal the treasure from the wicked troll. After all, he **was** king of the jungle and all kings should have their own treasure. And because Rex was not altogether a bad lion, he promised that he would share the treasure with the other animals, and the stranger too.

As the next few days went by Rex became more excited about stealing the treasure, boasting of his renowned strength and chanting his rap to anyone who'd listen. The stranger set about drawing Rex a map, as he said he had no desire, himself, to return to the castle of the wicked and cunning troll.

The day soon came for Rex to set off on his journey. To say that he was confident, well, let's just say that was an understatement. He had already planned what he was going to do with his share of the treasure. As he started to describe to the other animals the wonderful crown he was going to have made, a squeaky little voice interrupted him. He looked around him, in surprise, trying to work out where it was coming from. Suddenly he felt something tickling his giant paw. It was a small brown mouse, one of the smallest young rodents he'd ever seen. Rex stared at the mouse in amazement, at it's tiny paws and its little brown body

The mouse, who's name was Humphrey, cleared his tiny throat to speak. He explained to Rex that he and some of the other animals, Sid the Boa Constrictor and Madge and Mave the twin monkeys, would like to join him on his journey. They thought that they might be useful to him. At this, Rex threw his giant head back and laughed until his sides shook.

'Well,' he said, 'I can't stop you from coming with me but I can tell you now that you couldn't possibly be of any use to me, Rex, king of the jungle!'

The animals thanked him and promised that they would keep their distance and be sure not to get in the way.

So Rex, Humphrey, Sid, Madge and Mave set out on the arduous journey to the troll's castle. Rex was indeed fit and strong and the animals had to work very hard to keep up with him. It was just lucky for them that every so often he liked to stop and chant his little rap at some poor jungle creature who hadn't had the pleasure of hearing it before.

Finally, they arrived at the castle. It's walls were dark and crumbling and covered with creeping jungle plants but it was much smaller than they'd imagined. Rex smiled confidently and strode up to the castle gate. He let out a loud and mighty lion's roar.
'I am Rex, king of this jungle and I have come to steal your treasure, wicked troll!'

The animals, somewhat deafened by his mighty roar, hid behind a nearby bush.
'Do you think that was ssssuch a sssmart idea, announsssing his presssssence like that?' hissed Sid.
'Well, I'm sure he knows what he's doing,' squeaked Humphrey.
'Must do! Must do!' echoed Madge and Mave.

All of a sudden the castle gates swung open. There, in front of Rex, stood two small troll guards, dressed from head to toe in armour. Rex let out another frightening roar, picked the two trolls up with ease and banged their helmeted heads together. They fell to the floor, dazed.

'Well, that was easy,' he chuckled and was about to launch into his rap again when, thankfully, he thought better of it.
'I might as well get this over and done with,' he said to himself, 'I really can't see what the fuss is about. If this wicked troll is anything like his pathetic guards, then stealing the treasure should be a piece of cake.'

At that moment, he was interrupted by a thin wiry voice ahead of him.
'Come and get your precious treasure, mighty lion! But don't go thinking you'll be taking it away with you.'

Rex ran forward in the direction of the voice, eager to see who was talking to him. The other animals crept forward cautiously, being sure to keep themselves hidden. Suddenly, in front of Rex, was the biggest pile of treasure you could possibly imagine, especially if you're a lion and you haven't seen much treasure before anyway. The stranger had not been exaggerating when he had described the wonderful jewels and sparkling gold. No sooner had Rex taken in the beauty of the treasure than he noticed the wicked troll himself, small, wizened and mean looking.

'Let's see what good being king of the jungle does you now!' said the troll, laughing, and, before Rex could even think about chanting the first line of his favourite rap, a huge net fell on top of him, making it impossible for him to move.
'Now who's so strong and smart?' taunted the troll.
And as much as Rex struggled and roared, he could do nothing to free himself.

All of a sudden he remembered the other animals and, just as he was thinking that they had probably already fled in fright, he saw Madge and Mave appear from nowhere. Before the troll could say anything, they started doing somersaults, juggling rubies at the same time.
'Typical of those daft monkeys,' he thought, 'Showing off their tricks at a time like this!' but then he noticed Sid as well, who, unbeknown to the wicked troll was slowly but surely winding

his long body around the trolls legs.   And, when the troll realised he was stuck, it was too late for him to do anything about it.

'Come on! Come on!' shouted Madge and Mave in unison, 'Fill these bags with treasure, as quick as you can!'

'But I can't . . . . . ' Rex stopped mid sentence as he noticed Humphrey chewing away at the net, allowing him to step free. 'Come on, Rex,' squeaked Humphrey, 'We don't have any time to lose. And, by the way, I'll need a lift out of here,' he said, hopping onto Rex's back.

'I can't hold him forever,' hissed Sid, 'You'd better get going. I'll catch you up.'

So the animals grabbed the bags of treasure and quickly made their way back through the jungle. As they neared their home Sid caught up with them, still hissing with delight at how they'd got the better of the troll.

The animals excitedly told their friends how they'd managed to outsmart the wicked troll. Rex made a particular point of saying that he couldn't have done it without the help of the others. And, strangely enough, Rex's boasting had almost disappeared and he made up a new and very funky rap, telling of how he and his clever new friends had combined their talents to outwit the wicked troll.

Kryssy Hurley

After reading the story, ask the children what lesson they think the lion learnt and ask them what lesson we can learn from the story.

Finish by inviting a group of children to share some of their talents with the rest of the school.

EXAMPLE: Playing an instrument, dancing, showing badges achieved for swimming, etc.

NOTE ☐ This part of the assembly can be as brief or as long as you wish.

Finish the assembly with the following reflection.

REFLECTION

Let us give thanks for our own special talents and abilities and think about the ways in which we can make the most of them. Perhaps we have talents which we can use to help others. Maybe it is something as simple as being a good listener or a good friend. Whatever our talents, they are valuable and something for us to be proud of.

ADDITIONAL RESOURCES AND ACTIVITIES

> You could read the children the parable of the master who gave his three servants a number of gold or silver coins, before setting out on a journey, and then returning to see what use they had made of them. *The Parable of the Talents* St Matthew Chapter 25, New Testament, the Holy Bible.

> Read the fable *The Lion and the Three Bulls* * Aesop The Complete Fables, Penguin.
> > * Moral - Union is strength.

> You could hold a class talent show or celebration.

> The children could give talks about their various talents and hobbies, and photographs and information could be mounted as part of a wall display.

> The children could find out about the lives of talented people in different walks of life. e.g. sports world record holders, famous composers, musicians, actors and dancers, political and religious world leaders, etc. There are also some quirky achievements to be found in the Guiness Book of Records.

10. MOVING ON

PSHE LINK: FEELING POSITIVE ABOUT THEMSELVES
PREPARING FOR CHANGE

RESOURCES AND ORGANISATION

You will need:-

- 1 Spring bulb.

  EXAMPLE: daffodil bulb, tulip bulb.

- A collection of outdoor equipment.

- 1 Overhead transparency sheet and pen.

- A set of 14 Qualities and Attributes Cards written in class.*
  * or use the sample cards.

- 14 Preselected children to each take a piece of equipment off the Volunteer, read out and give their Qualities and Attributes Card.*
  * or children chosen on the day to read the sample cards.

- 1 Volunteer chosen on the day to carry items of equipment.

- 2 Small groups of preselected children who will soon be leaving the school - one group to read their memories of primary school and the other group to list their expectations for their next school.

WHAT TO DO

Start the assembly by reminding the children that the end of the school year is approaching, that Year 6 children are thinking about moving on to new schools and that other children in the school are getting ready to move up to a new class. Explain that in this assembly we shall be thinking about endings but also about moving on, to face new challenges and embrace new experiences.

Show the children the bulb and explain that when the flower dies down after blooming, it appears to be dead and finished, when really it is just waiting to grow again in the Spring. In the same way, the older children in the school are having to say good-bye to this school, as they come to the end of their time here. At the same time, they are about to start a new life at a different school. Children who are getting ready to join a new class are also about to face new challenges and possibly take on greater responsibility as they get older.

> At this point ask for a volunteer to come to the front.

Ask the children watching to suggest some equipment they think the child might need if he/she was about to set out on a long journey, let's say a journey by foot. Add that the weather may also be unpredictable and that there aren't any fast food restaurants or supermarkets on the way. As the children suggest items which might be useful, give them to the child to wear or carry.

NOTE ☐ Any items that you don't have to hand can be written down in a list on the overhead transparency.

SUGGESTED ITEMS OF EQUIPMENT

- walking boots
- hat
- coat
- back pack
- food
- water bottle
- compass
- binoculars
- umbrella
- portable tent
- sunglasses
- extra jumpers
- gloves
- maps
- torch
- sun cream
- insect repellent

- and any other appropriate pieces of outdoor equipment that you can find.

The volunteer will gradually become better equipped and may find, to the amusement of the children watching, that it is difficult to hold everything needed at once.

Explain to the children that our Year 6 children are not necessarily going to need such huge amounts of equipment to prepare them for secondary school, although they will obviously need some special equipment, but that they will certainly need to be equipped in other ways.

> Preselected children from Year 6 can then come up to the front and take a piece of equipment off the volunteer one at a time. As they do so, each one can give the volunteer a card instead with something which they think is important written on it.

NOTE ☐ These cards can come from earlier work done with Year 6 in class or you might prefer to use the sample Qualities and Attributes Cards.

SAMPLE QUALITIES AND ATTRIBUTES CARDS

good friends

confidence

a sense of adventure

a sense of humour

patience

a sense of what they want to achieve

the ability to make choices and think for themselves

tolerance

understanding

responsibility

a willingness to join in or to have a go

perseverance

friendliness

---

knowing where to go for help and advice

NOTE ☐ The children may come up with a list similar to this.

Explain that although these are not things that you can go out and buy, they are all things that we hope our school has helped to encourage in pupils, so that they can take on new challenges with confidence.

Moving to a new school or to a new area can be quite daunting and it is natural to have concerns and things you are worried about, but hopefully some of the above attitudes and qualities, along with support from family and friends, will make the journey a little easier.

Say that you are going to read a poem by Roger McGough about the way a child sees his/her first day at school.

FIRST DAY AT SCHOOL

A millionbillionwillion miles from home
Waiting for the bell to go. (To go where?)
Why are they all so big, other children?
So noisy? So much at home they
Must have been born in uniform.
Lived all their lives in playgrounds
Spent the years inventing games
That don't let me in. Games
That are rough, that swallow you up.

And the railings.
All around, the railings.
Are they to keep out wolves and monsters?
Things that carry off and eat children?
Things you don't take sweets from?
Perhaps they're to stop us getting out
Running away from the lessins. Lessin.
What does a lessin look like?
Sounds small and slimy.
They keep them in glassrooms.
Whole rooms made out of glass. Imagine.

I wish I could remember my name
Mummy said it would come in useful.
Like wellies. When there's puddles.
Lellowwellies. I wish she was here.
I think my name is sown on somewhere
Perhaps the teacher will read it for me.
Tea-cher. The one who makes the tea.

Roger McGough

First Day At School from You Tell me Poems
by Roger McGough and Michael Rosen (Kestrel, 1979)
Copyright © Roger McGough, 1979 Puffin Books.

At this point, a small group of Year 6 children can read some brief accounts of their memories of school.

NOTE ☐ These might include some very early memories or events in their school life which they feel they will remember for a long time.

Finally, another small group can read out a list of expectations i.e. some of the things which they are looking forward to doing at secondary school.

Finish the assembly with the following reflection.

REFLECTION

Let the children who are leaving us gather up all the good memories of their life at this school and wrap them around themselves like a warm patchwork quilt, colourful and familiar. Give them the confidence to face new challenges with enthusiasm, to make the most of their talents and to greet the world with a smile, a warm heart and an open mind.

ADDITIONAL RESOURCES AND ACTIVITIES

> Children could write about their memories of starting school.

> The children could read the story *The Velveteen Rabbit* by Margery Williams, Faber.

> The children could listen to creation stories from different faiths.

> The children could find out how different faiths view death and birth.

    EXAMPLE: Buddhist, Hindu, Christian, Muslim, etc.

> The children could pursue the general theme of moving on by discussing the times when changes occur in our lives.

> Invite a former pupil or a small group of former pupils from a secondary school to come and talk about how they coped with the changes.

> The children could write down their concerns and worries anonymously. Other children in the class could think of advice for these concerns which could then be discussed.

> Make a 'Leavers Memory Book' with a small photograph of each child. The children could then write down some of their memories together with their hopes for the future as they move on.

> Some of the leavers could be invited back at half-term to tell the present Year 6 children how they are enjoying secondary school.

11. MY SOCIETY

PSHE LINK: PREPARING TO PLAY AN ACTIVE ROLE AS A CITIZEN

RESOURCES AND ORGANISATION

You will need:-

- One preselected group of children to present work carried out in class on **Paradise Island**.

- A second preselected group of children to hold up their own pictures showing themselves surrounded by people and places that are important to them.

WHAT TO DO

society   1. any organised group of people joined together because of work, interests, etc.   2. all people, collectively regarded as constituting a community of related, interdependent individuals. 3. a group of persons regarded as having formed a single community, especially a distinct social or economic class.   4. the system or condition of living together as a community in such a group.   5. a group of persons regarded or regarding itself as a dominant class, usually because of wealth, birth, education, etc. 6. a group of animals or plants living together in a single environment.

Begin by asking the children watching what they understand by the word society. Many of them will probably mention the names of societies that they have heard of.

EXAMPLE: RSPCA. (Royal Society for the Prevention of Cruelty to Animals), RSPB (Royal Society for the Protection of Birds) NSPCC (National Society for the Prevention of Cruelty to Children), Woolwich Building Society, etc.

Explain that this is one definition of the word and that, any group or association of people with a common aim can form such a society.

Go on to explain that there is another meaning of the word society, one which is wider and which includes all of us, and that it describes the customs and organisation which make up our civilised nation.

Explain that societies are made up of physical things such as buildings and services and of the people which use them. Within society there are accepted ways of behaving, laws and beliefs. People within society also have certain rights and duties. They have different needs and a range of services need to be provided. There are also accepted systems within society.

EXAMPLE: the use of money, credit and debit cards, cheques.

There is a lot of interaction between all these aspects and people need to conform to certain ways of behaving. People are also dependent on each other and need to share skills. It would be very difficult to live a life completely outside society. Just as we are part of society, our school can be seen as a mini society, where people help and depend on each other.

Go on to say that some children have been thinking about the things which are needed to make a successful society, and that they have created their own society called **Paradise Island.**

Explain that the children were told that they had moved to Paradise Island because their own homeland had been destroyed in a natural disaster. They had arrived on the island, each with certain skills and with limited possessions. They had initially settled in different parts of the island. The task they had been given was, between them, to create a civilised society. They had to decide how they were going to make decisions, make a list of priorities of things to be done on the island and decide how they would share their talents and skills.

> At this point you may wish for some of the children to introduce themselves.

EXAMPLE: 'My name is Billie. I am thirty-four years old, I am a skilled carpenter and also have a good knowledge of plants.'

'My name is Jay. I am thirty-two years old, I am a trained teacher and love cooking.'

'My name is Ed. I am thirty-seven years old and have twin boys aged three. I am a doctor by profession and a keen angler.

The children can hold up a painted frieze/collage to show what their island looks like. They can then explain how they set about making the island a good place to live in, how they were able to make decisions, and the priority in which they decided to do things. They can also explain how they were able to co-operate with each other to create a society where people could live peacefully and happily.

EXAMPLE: agree living rules first, find or build some kind of shelter next, etc.

The second group of preselected children can then hold up some collage or photo-montage pictures they have made showing themselves surrounded by the people and places which are most important to them.

EXAMPLE: all the family at home together for a birthday party, seeing mum and dad in the audience at the school play, playing football with friends in the park, etc.

Finish the assembly with the following reflection.

REFLECTION

Help us to understand the value of living as part of society and to be active and responsible members. Let us appreciate those who provide services within our society and try to make a useful contribution ourselves.

ADDITIONAL RESOURCES AND ACTIVITIES

> The work on **Paradise Island** could be extended in greater detail and drama and role play could be used to explore relevant issues.

> Children could sit in a citizenship circle to discuss what they feel is needed to make up a civilised society.

> Children could think about the different needs of a range of groups within society.

EXAMPLE: The elderly, the young, families, etc.

A very useful teacher resource for activities of this kind is the pack *Partners in Rights*, published by Save the Children, which includes creative activities exploring rights and citizenship.

> Other useful teacher resources are the books *Coming Round* and *Holes*.
ISSUES: Breaking the law, telling lies, helping others, loyalty.
Coming Round by Anthony Lishak see recommended book list in Introducing Citizenship by Don Rowe, A & C Black
ISSUES: Justice, power, trust, etc.
Holes by Louis Sachar, Bloomsbury.

> The children could look at maps to find the symbols that are used to designate places of worship.

EXAMPLE: a cross represents Christianity and a crescent moon represents Islam. The importance of religious festivals in society, the reasons for the festivals and their main features could also be investigated.

Christmas
Christianity

• **Celebrating the birth of Jesus Christ.**
Church services, Christmas meal, cards and gifts.

Raksha Bandhan

Hinduism

• **Shows brothers and sisters they are important to each other**
Rakhi Ceremony

Ramadan

Islam

• **Fasting helps Muslims to obey God and to remember poor people who are hungry.**
Fasting, special prayers.

Pesach
Judaism

• **Remembering the story of Pesach**
The Seder Meal, reading from the Hagadah.

12. FAIR TRADE

PSHE LINK: PREPARING TO PLAY AN ACTIVE ROLE
AS A CITIZEN

see 2a, 2e, 2h and 2j
from National Curriculum PSHE guidelines

RESOURCES AND ORGANISATION

You will need:-

- 2 Shopping baskets containing shopping.

  NOTE ☐ One Basket must contain goods marked with the
  Fair Trade Mark. The other basket must contain
  identical or similar goods without the Fair Trade
  Mark.

  EXAMPLE: coffee, chocolate bar, tea, bananas, etc.

- 2 Flip charts.

- 1 Set of brightly coloured Vocabulary Cards to stick up on
  one of the flip charts.

VOCABULARY CARDS

developed world

developing world

third world country

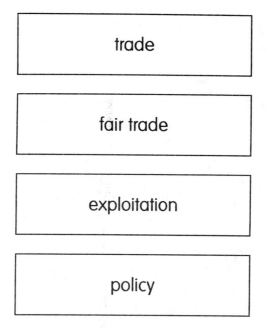

- A bunch of bananas, a box and 100 pennies for **The Banana Game.**

- 2 Sets of Trade Statement Cards for the supermarket activity and 2 flip charts.

- 10 Children - preselected or chosen on the day to play **The Banana Game.**

- 4 Children - preselected or chosen on the day to take part in the **Fair Supermarket Challenge.**

WHAT TO DO

Start by showing the children two baskets full of food from a supermarket. Hold up a selection of items from each basket and ask the children if they can see any differences between the contents of each basket.

NOTE ☐ As the items are identical or similar to look at the children will find it difficult to spot an obvious difference.

Go on to explain to them that the one basket contains goods which were produced as a result of fair trade. Ask if any of them know what fair trade is.

Using the brightly coloured vocabulary cards, explain the meanings in your own words using these definitions as a guide.

developed world
- rich countries that have developed economically, socially and politically after emergence into statehood.

developing world
- poor counties that are developing better economic and social conditions.

third world country
- a developing country of Asia, Africa and Latin America.

trade
- buying and selling between nations

fair trade
- buying and selling between nations in a fair manner.

exploitation
- taking advantage of people/a situation for personal gain.

policy
- a principal, plan or course of action adopted by a government organisation, business or individual.

Show the children what the Fair Trade Mark looks like and point it out on some of the food items. Explain that it is possible to buy products such as coffee, chocolate and bananas which have been produced by companies which have a Fair Trade policy.

Explain that the richer northern countries tend to be favoured by international trade rules and prices of goods frequently fluctuate wildly resulting in low wages and no job security for those in poorer countries. The richer northern countries depend on goods from the poorer southern countries and those countries, in turn, rely on being able to sell goods to the north. This is called interdependence. Fair trade ensures that there is justice and that the poorer countries are not treated unfairly.

interdependence dependence on each other or one another, mutual dependence.

The Fair Trade policy guarantees small farmers better prices and enables them to cover the cost of production, no matter how low the world market price goes.

The Fair Trade Foundation encourages fair treatment for small farmers, plantation and factory workers and children in third world countries.

Explain that you are going to tell them about five of the terms and conditions which the Fair Trade Foundation encourages.

NOTE □ You may like to read these terms and conditions out or you might prefer to hold up cards with them written on.

FAIR TRADE FOUNDATION TERMS AND CONDITIONS

• Small scale farmers can be part of a democratic organisation.

• Plantation and factory workers are given decent wages and living conditions.

• There is no child labour.

• Programmes are initiated which encourage care of the environment.

• Advance payment is given to farmers.

> Continue by inviting ten children to play The Banana Game.

THE BANANA GAME

Explain to the children that The Banana Game demonstrates that what is convenient for some people can be unfair to others. Explain to the selected children that they each represent someone who is involved in the production or selling of bananas. Show the children a bunch of bananas which can be bought in the shops for £1.00 [100 pence]. Each child will take on one of the following roles:

- Grower
- Insurer
- Shipper
- Ripener
- Packer
- Docker
- Exporter
- Transporter
- Retailer
- Shopper

These children can stand in a line as you explain to the children watching who they represent.

NOTE ☐ The children could all hold up cards stating their role or the cards could be hung around their necks.

The bananas can be passed along the line, from the grower to the shopper, as you explain each person's role. The shopper must then pay for the bananas, putting the one hundred pennies in the box. The box is then passed from person to person, back along the line for them to take out their share of the money.

- The Retailer begins by taking out 32p.

- The Transporter, the Exporter, the Docker and the Packer take out 26p between them.

- The Ripener takes out 18p.

- The Shipper and Insurer take out 12p between them.

- And the Grower is left with 12p.

the Banana Game by Steve Pratchett
for Christian Aid

At this point you can ask the children how fair they think the division of money was.

> Continue by inviting two pairs of children up to represent two large supermarkets, **FOODWAY** and **FRESHBURY.**

FAIR SUPERMARKET CHALLENGE

Explain that you are going to give them a selection of cards, showing a range of statements, and you would like them to select five cards which they feel have statements which they think ought to be included in their supermarket's Fair Trade policy. Give each pair a set of ten Trade Statement Cards:

TRADE STATEMENT CARDS

TRADE STATEMENT CARDS

We will guarantee to pay a minimum price which covers the cost of production.

1

TRADE STATEMENT CARDS

We will only trade with producers who provide their workers with decent housing, wages and working conditions.

2

TRADE STATEMENT CARDS

We will pay in advance so that small producer organisations do not fall into debt.

3

TRADE STATEMENT CARDS

We will form contracts which allow long term planning.

4

TRADE STATEMENT CARDS

We will encourage the use of better equipment and give advice on methods of growing and types of crops.

5

TRADE STATEMENT CARDS

We don't mind if child labour is used because it means the goods will be cheaper.

6

TRADE STATEMENT CARDS

We aren't interested in whether the workers have to work very long hours. We will leave decisions of that kind to the producer.

7

TRADE STATEMENT CARDS

We may cancel an order with short notice if we can get a cheaper price elsewhere.

8

TRADE STATEMENT CARDS

We are not interested in environmental sustainability.

9

TRADE STATEMENT CARDS

We will pay the land owners direct and let them decide how much or how little they wish to pay the workers.

10

Give each pair a few minutes to decide which cards they wish to choose for their Fair Trade policy. They can then stick their selection up on their flip chart.

> Ask the children for a show of hands to vote for the Fair Supermarket of the year.

Congratulate the winner. Ask the children watching if they agree with all the selections. Discuss the statements on the cards and talk about why some of them would not form part of a Fair Trade policy.

Go on to suggest that the children may wish to do some research on companies which have a Fair Trade policy or look out for the Fair Trade Mark on products and try to find out about them by reading the labels in their local supermarkets.

EXAMPLE:

Fairtrade statement: Waitrose Fairtrade bananas are grown on small, certified family farms, on the lush Caribbean island of St Lucia.

Fairtrade statement: Percol™ coffee - We want you to enjoy this coffee but not at the expense of the people who grow it or the environment it's grown in.
THIS COFFEE IS FAIRY TRADED.
The small scale producers who grow this coffee benefit directly from its sale under criteria set down by the Fairtrade Foundation.

Finish the assembly with the following reflection.

REFLECTION

Help us to understand issues such as fair trade, allocation of resources and economic choices. Help us to understand other people's experiences and realise that we can make decisions which, in turn, affect others.

ADDITIONAL RESOURCES AND ACTIVITIES

> Children could run a Fair Trade school shop.

> Children could organise a Fair Trade coffee morning, where parents can taste coffee and chocolate produced by companies such as Café Direct.

> The children could use the internet to research different countries and the food they produce.

> The children could conduct consumer surveys to find out how aware people are of Fair Trade issues.

> The children could collect Fairtrade statements, packaging and labels and pictures from travel brochures, etc and make a montage frieze.

> Useful web sites include:
  www.fairtrade.org.uk, www.oxfam.org.uk and
  www.cafedirect.co.uk.

> *Europlus*, a colourful free activity book suitable for key stages 2 & 3 takes a look at the countries wishing to join the European Union and can be used to explore aspects of citizenship.
  Europlus, published by the European Commission
  Representation in the United Kingdom, produced by
  Perceptor Ltd. tel: 020 7307 7420
  email: engage@perceptor.uk.com

ADDITIONAL TITLES

All books may be ordered direct from:

DRAMATIC LINES   PO BOX 201   TWICKENHAM   TW2 5RQ
freephone: 0800 5429570   fax: 020 8296 9503

MONOLOGUES

THE SIEVE AND OTHER SCENES
Heather Stephens
ISBN 0 9522224 0 X

The Sieve contains unusual short original monologues valid for junior acting examinations. The material in The Sieve has proved popular with winning entries worldwide in drama festival competitions. Although these monologues were originally written for the 8-14 year age range they have been used by adult actors for audition and performance pieces. Each monologue is seen through the eyes of a young person with varied subject matter including tough social issues such as fear, 'Television Spinechiller', senile dementia, 'Seen Through a Glass Darkly' and withdrawal from the world in 'The Sieve'.   Other pieces include: 'A Game of Chicken', 'The Present', 'Balloon Race' and a widely used new adaptation of Hans Christian Andersen's 'The Little Match Girl' in monologue form.

CABBAGE AND OTHER SCENES
Heather Stephens
ISBN 0 9522224 5 0

Following the success of The Sieve, Heather Stephens has written an additional book of monologues with thought provoking and layered subject matter valid for junior acting examinations.   The Cabbage monologues were originally written for the 8-14 year age range but have been used by adult actors for audition and performance pieces.   The Aberfan slag heap disaster issues are graphically confronted in 'Aberfan Prophecy' and 'The Surviving Twin' whilst humorous perceptions of life are observed by young people in 'The Tap Dancer' and 'Cabbage'.   Other pieces include: 'The Dinner Party Guest', 'Nine Lives' and a new adaptation of Robert Browning's 'The Pied Piper' seen through the eyes of the crippled child.

ALONE IN MY ROOM ORIGINAL MONOLOGUES
Ken Pickering
ISBN 0 9537770 0 6

This collection of short original monologues includes extracts from the author's longer works in addition to the classics. Provocative issues such as poverty and land abuse are explored in 'One Child at a Time', 'The Young Person Talks' and 'Turtle Island' with adaptations from 'Jane Eyre', Gulliver's Travels' and 'Oliver Twist' and well loved authors including Dostoyevsky. These monologues have a wide variety of applications including syllabus recommendation for various acting examinations. Each monologue has a brief background description and acting notes.

DUOLOGUES

PEARS

Heather Stephens
ISBN 0 9522224 6 9

Heather Stephens has written layered, thought provoking and unusual short original duologues to provide new material for speech and drama festival candidates in the 8-14 year age range. The scenes have also been widely used for junior acting examinations and in a variety of school situations and theatrical applications. Challenging topics in Pears include the emotive issues of child migration, 'Blondie', 'The Outback Institution' and bullying 'Bullies', other scenes examine friendship, 'The Best of Friends', 'The Row' and envy, 'Never the Bridesmaid'. New duologue adaptations of part scenes from the classic play, 'Peace' by Aristophanes and 'Oliver Twist' by Charles Dickens are also included.

TOGETHER NOW ORIGINAL DUOLOGUES

Ken Pickering
ISBN 0 9537770 1 4

This collection of short duologues includes extracts from Ken Pickering's longer works together with new original pieces. The variety of experiences explored in the scenes are those which we can all easily identify with such as an awkward situation, 'You Tell Her', and the journey of self knowledge in 'Gilgamesh' whilst pieces such as 'Mobile phones', 'Sales' and 'Food' observe realistic situations in an interesting and perceptive way. Other duologues are based on well known stories including 'Snow White' and 'The Pilgrim's Progress'. Each piece has a brief background description and acting notes and the scenes have syllabus recommendation for a number of examination boards as well as a wide variety of theatrical and school applications.

MONOLOGUES AND DUOLOGUES

SHAKESPEARE THE REWRITES

Claire Jones
ISBN 0 9522224 8 5

A collection of short monologues and duologues for female players. The scenes are from rewrites of Shakespeare plays from 1670 to the present day written by authors seeking to embellish original texts for performances, to add prequels or sequels or to satisfy their own very personal ideas about production. This material is fresh and unusual and will provide exciting new audition and examination material. Comparisons with the original Shakespeare text are fascinating and this book will provide a useful contribution to Theatre Study work from GCSE to beyond 'A' level. Contributors include James Thurber (Macbeth) Arnold Wesker (Merchant of Venice) and Peter Ustinov (Romanoff and Juliet). The collection also includes a most unusual Japanese version of Hamlet.

SCENES

JELLY BEANS

Joseph McNair Stover
ISBN 0 9522224 7 7

The distinctive style and deceptively simple logic of American writer Joseph McNair Stover has universal appeal with scenes that vary in tone from whimsical to serious and focus on young peoples relationships in the contemporary world. The collection of 10-15 minute original scenes for 2, 3 and 4 players is suitable for 11 year olds through to adult. Minimal use of sets and props makes pieces ideal for group acting examinations, classroom drama, assemblies and various other theatrical applications and have been used with success at Young Writers Workshops to teach the elements of script writing and dramatic development.

ONE ACT PLAYS

WILL SHAKESPEARE SAVE US!
WILL SHAKESPEARE SAVE THE KING!

Paul Nimmo
ISBN 0 9522224 1 8

Two versatile plays in which famous speeches and scenes from Shakespeare are acted out as part of a comic story about a bored king and his troupe of players. These plays are suitable for the 11-18 year age range and have been produced with varying ages within the same cast and also performed by adults to a young audience. The plays can be produced as a double bill, alternatively each will stand on its own, performed by a minimum cast of 10 without a set, few props and modern dress or large cast, traditional set and costumes. The scripts are ideal for reading aloud by classes or groups and provide an excellent introduction to the works of Shakespeare. Both plays have been successfully performed on tour and at the Shakespeare's Globe in London.

SUGAR ON SUNDAYS AND OTHER PLAYS

Andrew Gordon
ISBN 0 9522224 3 4

A collection of six one act plays bringing history alive through drama. History is viewed through the eyes of ordinary people and each play is packed with details about everyday life, important events and developments of the period. The plays can be used as classroom drama, for school performances and group acting examinations and can also be used as shared texts for the literacy hour. The plays are suitable for children from Key Stage 2 upwards and are 40-50 minutes in length and explore Ancient Egypt, Ancient Greece, Anglo-Saxon and Viking Times, Victorian Britain and the Second World War. A glossary of key words helps to develop children's historical understanding of National Curriculum History Topics and the plays provide opportunities for children to enjoy role play and performance.

TEENAGE PLAYS

X-STACY
Margery Forde
ISBN 0 9522224 9 3

Margery Forde's powerful play centres on the rave culture and illicit teenage drug use and asks tough questions about family, friends and mutual responsibilities. The play has proved hugely successful in Australia and this English edition is published with extensive teachers' notes by Helen Radian, Lecturer of Drama at Queensland University of Technology, to enrich its value for the secondary school classroom, PSHE studies, English and drama departments.

WHAT IS THE MATTER WITH MARY JANE?
Wendy Harmer
ISBN 0 9522224 4 2

This monodrama about a recovering anorexic and bulimic takes the audience into the painful reality of a young woman afflicted by eating disorders. The play is based on the personal experience of actress Sancia Robinson and has proved hugely popular in Australia. It is written with warmth and extraordinary honesty and the language, humour and style appeal to current youth culture. A study guide for teachers and students is included in this English edition ensuring that the material is ideal for use in the secondary school classroom and for PSHE studies, drama departments in schools and colleges in addition to amateur and professional performance.

MUSICAL PLAYS

THREE CHEERS FOR MRS BUTLER
adapted by Vicky Ireland
ISBN 0 9537770 4 9

This versatile musical play about everyday school life is for anyone who has ever been to school. It features the poems and characters created by Allan Ahlberg with songs by Colin Matthews and Steven Markwick and was first performed at the Polka Theatre for Children, London. The two acts of 40 minutes each can be performed by children, adults or a mixture of both and the play can be produced with a minimum cast of 7 or a large cast of any size.

INTRODUCING OSCAR
The Selfish Giant & The Happy Prince
Veronica Bennetts
ISBN 0 9537770 3 0

Oscar Wilde's timeless stories for children have been chosen for adaptation because of the rich opportunities offered for imaginative exploration and the capacity to vividly illuminate many aspects of the human condition. The original dialogue, lyrics and music by Veronica Bennetts can be adapted and modified according to the needs of the pupils and individual schools or drama groups. The Selfish Giant runs for 25 minutes and The Happy Prince for 1 hour 15 minutes. Both musicals can be used for examinations and are ideal for end of term productions, for drama groups and primary and secondary schools.

DRAMA LESSONS IN ACTION

Antoinette Line
ISBN 0 9522224 2 6

Resource material suitable for classroom and assembly use for teachers of junior and secondary age pupils. Lessons are taught through improvisation. These are not presented as 'model lessons' but provide ideas for adaptation and further development. The lessons include warm-up and speech exercises and many themes are developed through feelings such as timidity, resentfulness, sensitivity and suspicion. The material can be used by groups of varying sizes and pupils are asked to respond to interesting texts from a diverse selection of well known authors including: Roald Dahl, Ogden Nash, Ted Hughes, Michael Rosen, Oscar Wilde and John Betjeman.

AAARGH TO ZIZZ 135 DRAMA GAMES

Graeme Talboys
ISBN 0 9537770 5 7

This valuable resource material has been created by a drama teacher and used mostly in formal drama lessons but also in informal situations such as clubs and parties. The games are extremely flexible, from warm up to cool down, inspiration to conclusion and from deadly serious to purest fun and the wide variety ranges from laughing and rhythm activities to building a sentence and word association. Games such as Do You Like Your Neighbour? could be used as part of a PSHE programme together with many of the activities connected with 'fair play'. The games are easily adapted and each has notes on setting up details of straightforward resources needed. All this material has been used with a wide range of young people in the 10 - 18 year age range.

DRAMA•DANCE•SINGING
TEACHER RESOURCE BOOK

edited by John Nicholas
ISBN 0 9537770 2 2

Phillip Schofield has written the foreword for this collection of drama, dance and singing lesson activities that have been drawn from a bank of ideas used by the Stagecoach Theatre Arts Schools teachers. Lessons include speech and drama exercises, games and improvisations often developed as a response to emotions. Dance activities include warm-ups, basic dance positions, improvisations, versatile dance exercises and routines while singing activities help to develop rhythm and notation as well as providing enjoyable games to develop the voice. Activities can be adapted for large or small group use and are suitable for 6 - 16 year olds in a fun yet challenging way.